# Victorian Childhood

By Susan P. Casteras

*Assistant Curator of Paintings*

*Yale Center for British Art*

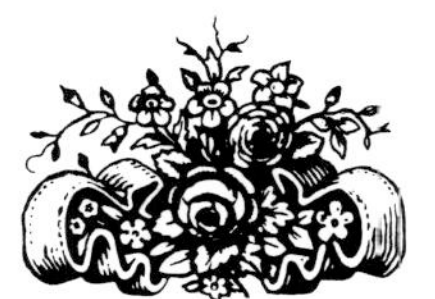

*Paintings selected from*

*the FORBES Magazine Collection*

*by Christopher Forbes*

HARRY N. ABRAMS, INC., PUBLISHER, NEW YORK

## AUTHOR'S ACKNOWLEDGMENTS

Neither this book nor the accompanying exhibition would have been possible without the guidance and encouragement of Christopher Forbes, whom I thank above all for his help in this undertaking as well as for his generous support of the Victorian Society in America and other Victorian projects. His knowledge and taste have shaped the exceptional contents of the FORBES Magazine Collection, which in the realm of Victorian art has resulted in astonishing breadth and quality. Few Americans have collected in this field on any scale, and the FORBES Magazine holdings are unique in this respect in this country.

Among others whose assistance has been invaluable I wish to single out Margaret Kelly, Curator of the FORBES Magazine Collection. At the Yale Center for British Art, Duncan Robinson, Malcolm Cormack, Constance Clement, and Betty Muirden were all very helpful. I am also grateful to Betty Elzea, Malcolm Warner, and Leslie Williams for their suggestions on various scholarly points concerning individual paintings. Lastly, on a personal note, I would like to dedicate this book to Louise C. Ash, who first opened my eyes to the aesthetic value and beauty of things associated with a Victorian childhood.

S.P.C.

*Project Director:* Darlene Geis

*Designer:* Carol Robson

*Published on the occasion of the exhibition at the Yale Center for British Art, New Haven, Connecticut*

LC# 86–71294



Printed in Japan

# CONTENTS

# THE VICTORIAN CULT OF CHILDHOOD

The popularity of sentimental genre pictures in Victorian England is well established, and narrative paintings with nineteenth-century subject matter were produced by some of the most important artists of the period. Filled with incident and detail, such paintings depended upon a mixture of stylistic exactitude and calculated emotion to achieve their success with viewers. As one critic wrote about this type of art in *The Art Journal* in 1863, "England, happy in her homes . . . and peaceful in her snug firesides, is equally fortunate in a School of Art sacred to the relations of domestic life. From the prince to the peasant . . . the same sentiments—love of God, charity to neighbours, duties of parents and child—these principles and emotions . . . have found earnest and literal expression through domestic pictures, which, both by their number and mastery, may almost claim to be national."

This fascination with what were called "cabinet domestic pictures" was in part a reflection of the growth and patronage of the middle class, for such narrative art found a sympathetic and ready market among buyers. Accordingly, recognizable truth of sentiment—whether of pathos or humor—was a paramount consideration, and an artist's concept was supposed to stay within the parameters of socially acceptable themes. Even trivial incidents were popular with bourgeois patrons, and pleasant as well as unpleasant subjects were to be "neatly turned, . . . sparkling . . . plain, perspicuous, and persuasive," as *The Art Journal* pointed out in 1864.

Given these criteria, one of the most universal themes, yet one that was inherently national, was that of the child, and in many respects the Victorian era (1837–1901) heralded a golden age of childhood, at least for the middle and upper classes. The demographics of the years from 1800 to 1914 also reveal that one third of the British population during those years consisted of children under the age of fourteen. In terms of literature, numerous Victorian authors produced important publications just for juvenile readers, including Charles Dodgson, Edward Lear, Charlotte Yonge, Margaret Scott Gatty, Charles Kingsley, Captain Frederick Maryatt, Julia Horatio Ewing, George Macdonald, and Mary Stewart Molesworth. Their contributions ranged from fairy tales to poetry and moral homilies, and concurrent with this rich flow of literature was a parallel tide of children's magazines, providing still another channel for instruction and pleasure. During this same period illustrators such as Beatrix Potter, Richard Doyle, John Tenniel, Eleanor Boyle, Walter Crane, and Kate Greenaway also contributed to this flourishing children's literature. In addition, toy manufacturers capitalized upon a juvenile audience abetted by parental indulgence, attesting in still another way to the growing attention being focused on Victorian children.

Although children were often important protagonists in Victorian literature and art, adult values clearly underlie the material and reinforce prevailing behavior and attitudes toward discipline, love, industriousness, child-rearing practices, and the approved roles of the sexes. While Victorian children's magazines were intended primarily for youngsters, paintings of the same period that dealt with themes of childhood were created almost exclusively for the enjoyment and emotions of adults, typically for exhibition at the Royal Academy or similar institutions. In both fiction and art, some subjects were clearly idealized, while others were presented as more realistic reflections of everyday life. In books and magazines, reading fare was tailored for each sex, with adventure tales reserved for boys and much tamer domestic stories designated for girls. While representations of children in a genre context certainly existed in earlier (i.e., Dutch seventeenth-century) art, the Victorian painters seized upon the topic of daily life with renewed and decidedly British zeal.

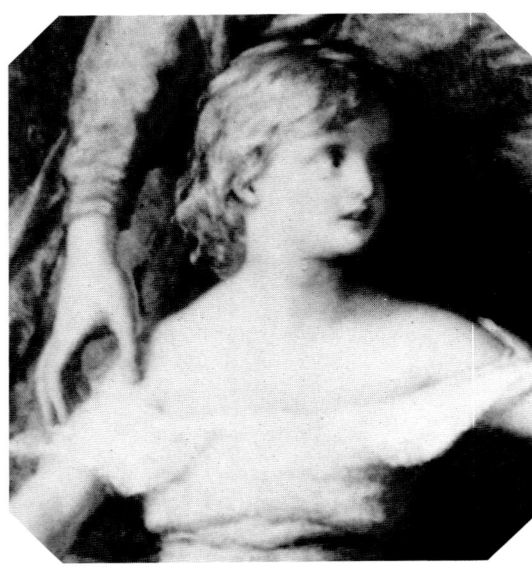

Detail from *Train Up a Child*

There are many categories that could be singled out for analysis in the Victorian representation of childhood, but among the most significant are those concerning the child's role within the family sphere, as a moral force in society, and his or her functions in the setting of home, school, work, and play. Of course, the degree of didacticism conveyed by a picture could be subtle or overt, the latter exemplified in William Mulready's *Train Up a Child* (Pl. 18), where the burden of charity falls upon a little boy whose moral teachings come directly from his mother. Sometimes the message that modern viewers receive is different from what might have been originally intended, so that we may detect both hypocrisy and sugar-coated indifference in the treatment of the impoverished urban child in particular. It must be remembered, however, that the majority of such works were produced for a bourgeois audience that wanted pathos but not pain from narrative pictures, and certainly not a lecture underscoring their own lack of sensitivity to the plight of the downtrodden. At the same time, it is worth pointing out that in the realm of literature, paradoxically, Dickens, Trollope, and George Eliot were able to criticize the world for their middle-class readers, who may have preferred reading about such miseries to seeing the same subjects in paintings.

One theme that often startles modern viewers (who deem the subject a more forbidden one than sex, the Victorian taboo) is death, particularly the portrayal of a dead or dying child. The terrible reality of a high infant mortality rate, and that of older children who succumbed to such disorders as scarlet fever or diphtheria, cast its shadow over the entire Victorian era and created especially tragic statistics among the lower classes. Accordingly, the sick or expiring child is a recurrent figure—sometimes portrayed as an embodiment of Christian endurance and acceptance, at other times as a victim of poverty. The parental vigil was a kindred theme that proved quite pervasive in art, with all classes affected by a visit from the Grim Reaper. Lower-class protagonists appear, for example, in Frank Holl's 1775 *Doubtful Hope* (Pl. 7) and Thomas Faed's 1868 *Worn Out* (Pl. 5), while upper-class characters face a similar lugubrious moment in Thomas Brooks's 1863 *Resignation* (Pl. 37), where a youngster's struggle for survival has been lost and the stoicism and faith of the child must now be inherited by the parents. A related image concerns the often mawkish "ascension" into heaven of the innocent child, a moment meant to be comforting to the bereaved family but nonetheless a difficult transition to manage pictorially with any credibility, seen in paintings such as George Hicks's 1890 *A Cloud with a Silver Lining* (Pl. 39).

Interestingly, while middle-class mothers and fathers are often characterized as being emotionally distant from their offspring, this strand of deathbed imagery in art suggests how much spectators must have liked being reminded of the preciousness of life and of the children in the family. In addition, rural parents—fathers in particular—often are portrayed, as in the Faed painting, in quite a positive light, filled with paternal affection and solicitude and not at all the unapproachable paterfamilias. On a happier note, a heightened esteem for children and childhood is also evident in pictures that celebrate parental pride in a young one's existence, as in Michael Halliday's 1858 *The Blind Basket-Maker with his First Child* (Pl. 16) and Hubert von Herkomer's 1887 *The First Born* (Pl. 35).

In art as in real life, there were strict divisions between activities deemed proper for girls and those that were permitted for boys. In Victorian novels by Dickens as well as by less eminent writers, the middle-class girl was delineated as rather one-dimensional: cloyingly sweet, pious, helpful and self-effacing to an inordinate degree, and otherwise a "goody-goody." In truth, young females were urged to emulate idealized standards of submissiveness, meekness, and respectability, with the result that they were more often dependent, decorative, and vapid rather than feisty or independent. In fact, they typically served in art and in fiction as youthful versions of Coventry Patmore's "angels in the house," mimicking the alleged moral and spiritual superiority of their mothers. This veneration of girls as quasi-heavenly beings is apparent in both Frederick Sandys's *At Vespers*, about 1860 (Pl. 8) and Thomas Gotch's 1896 *Alleluya* (Pl. 38), where the female singers—whether mortal or celestial—are so demure and devout that they are all but transported by the sacred music. Their angelic counterparts in Arthur Hughes's 1867 *A Birthday Picnic* (Pl. 6) are similarly beatific, immobile, and blandly pretty.

The sister played a vital role in the Victorian family and was constantly encouraged to be a paragon of usefulness and selflessness and always to place male needs above her own. In such a middle-class atmosphere of virtue and altruism there was little evidence of female aggression, pluck, or initiative, and this was mirrored in the period's pictorial representations. While the misbehaving boy was a staple in Victorian art and literature, the mischievous girl is seen infrequently. Even later in the century, when girls' lives became freer both in terms of educational and athletic possibilities, these stereotypes persisted. While girls' books moved away from a heavy-handed moralism extolling feminine self-sacrifice early in the Victorian era to a portrayal in later years of a more self-reliant and capable girl in pursuit of vigorous sport, adventure, and fun, there was less evidence of this change in paintings. And although tomboy-taming was a recurrent theme in girls' fiction, there were few hints in art that such hoydenish girls existed. There were, of course, some "bad" girls in Victorian novels, but these tended to be contrived villainesses who were as naughty as the heroines were virtuous; the closest analogy to them in art is found in the common pairing of dark- and light-haired "rivals" or juxtapositions of rich and poor or idle and industrious young females. While the Victorian schoolboy was a stock character in art, his female counterpart was rare, although fictional accounts often made school a place where girls could enjoy some freedom and fun away from the restrictions of home.

One obvious aspect of female role-playing reflected in art involved the inculcation of social values of wife and mother; the image of the maternal little girl taking care of her siblings, pet, or doll was commonplace. Girls with gentle, though sometimes sulky, expressions taking care of others or engaged in domestic tasks like needlework or gardening were omnipresent characters in Victorian painting, and so too was the beautiful, idle young girl suspended in a moment of exquisite leisure or private reverie. Sometimes to the modern viewer there seems to be more than a hint of latent sensuality in such portrayals, just as there are ambivalent undertones in Lewis Carroll's famous photographs of nude young females and in paintings of "baby odalisques" or childish courting scenes. This sensuous undercurrent may be related to the fact that up to the end of the century the age of consent for a female to wed was only twelve or thirteen. It also underscores the fact that the ideal Victorian lady was praised for basically infantile qualities; thus, the perfect woman was girlish, and the perfect girl was womanly, and these mingling traits are conveyed in the literature and paintings of the time. Even when the sexes are portrayed together, girls are generally assigned the more passive roles as observer, nurturer, peacemaker, or mother surrogate, and not intrepid explorer, inventor, or resourceful problem-solver. There are paintings where girls do join in livelier fun—as in Alexander Burr's 1888 *Blind Man's Buff* (Pl. 11), but for the most part, a girl is depicted as a modest and helpless captive of the parlor until late in the century, when the emancipated "New Woman" had at least some small impact on the advent of the liberated "New Girl" and her more athletic and intellectual interests.

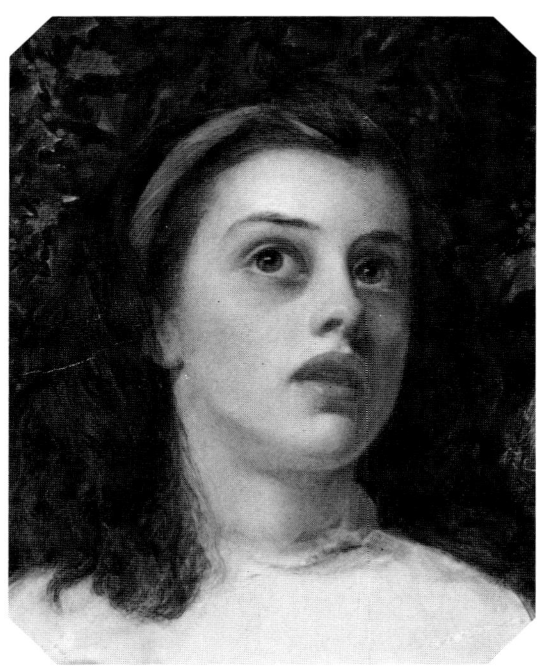

Detail from *At Vespers*

Ironically, depictions of the lower-class female often gave her more variety and versatility (because of fewer limitations on her conduct—aside from poverty—one assumes), but the results were usually just as saturated with treacly sentimentality. There were myriad representations of young farm girls and rural laborers, all well-fed and rosy-cheeked and embodying many of the same moral attributes as their more affluent sisters. In Victorian paintings female subservience and winsomeness are both prized traits, as in John Everett Millais's 1888 *For the Squire* (cover illustration), for example. Here a soulful little blond girl brings a letter to the all-powerful male squire, and her image is exploited for every ounce of sweetness. Similarly, the picturesque vulnerability of female orphans was also seized upon by Victorian authors and artists, who used their subjects' helplessness and prettiness as key ingredients in their appeal to audiences. Even those young girls who were trapped in a brutal urban environment were generally viewed as picturesque and plaintive—not broken or destitute—victims of the street. They were seen as objects of pity and even amusement, as in Augustus E. Mulready's numerous paintings of flowersellers and street vendors, without any intention of pointing an indicting finger at the middle-class patron who may have ignored the actual existence and needs of these people in reality.

While respectable Victorian girls in art are invariably shown upholding the status quo of their class, greater latitude seems to have been granted boys, and depictions of them, accordingly, seem more complex and varied. At its most serious, even divine, level, the subgenre of the "boy hero" was accorded a place of honor in contemporary paintings. The perfect child was Christ himself, and Holman Hunt and others sometimes treated the biblical subject of the young Jesus. (Themes of "holy girlhood" were much less common.) Beyond paintings of holy children, there was a pictorial preoccupation with producing boyhood portraits of famous men, and the precocious male genius or historical figure recurs notably in Edward Ward's 1849 *Benjamin West's First Effort in Art*, Charles Compton's 1849 *An Incident in the Life of Benjamin West*, William Dyce's 1857 *Titian's First Essay in Colour*, John Phillip's 1865 *The Early Career of Murillo*, and Marcus Stone's 1871 *The Royal Nursery, 1538*.

In a secular context, while the brash or truculent girl was unthinkable in a typical Victorian genre picture, the lively and disruptive male hooligan or truant—as in J. W. Nicol's *Cause* and *Effect* pictures (Pl. 30) and several paintings by William Mulready—was an omnipresent creature. The typical locale for young male misconduct was the schoolroom and the schoolyard, places where boys were encouraged to be aggressive and willful. One of the striking features of works in this category, such as John Faed's 1849 *Boyhood* (back cover) or John Morgan's 1869 *The Fight* (Pl. 2), is the amount of violence they could convey, for physical abuse to and by children was clearly quite acceptable to the Victorians under certain circumstances. While the home may have endorsed rigid rules and even corporal punishment for misdemeanors, the public (private, to Americans) schools of Britain could be, by many accounts, veritable hotbeds of sadism and cruelty.

Artists like Thomas Webster rarely showed young bullies acting in a brutal manner, as did their often ineffectual schoolmasters, who nevertheless seem more laughable than intimidating. In the educational system of nineteenth-century England, the code dictated that it was unsporting to be a spy or a "snitch," and in dormitory life as in organized field games it was desirable to acquire traits such as fairness and loyalty. Thus, the boys who cavort in Matthias Robinson's 1863 *The Battle of the Bolsters* (Pl. 9) are expected not to inform on one another, in spite of the impending danger suggested by the cane-brandishing male teacher at the threshold. Team spirit and the importance of enduring physical and psychological pain were all part of the Victorian cult of manliness, and attitudes toward aggression, justice, sportsmanship, and the need for a healthy body and mind were all projected by novels such as the renowned *Tom Brown's Schooldays* series. Just as portrayals of the sedentary and insular activity of girls in the home suggest the Victorian definition of femininity, so too do the depictions of bellicose and even ruthless schoolboys convey several layers of meaning about masculinity and the associated rites of passage.

Boys, however, could undermine authority as a way of learning to become leaders of men, while girls were rarely given an equal opportunity to exercise their judgment or will. Ultimately, the games and lessons learned on and off the proverbial playing field were thought to serve as preparations for adult responsibilities such as soldiering, and this is certainly part of the message of James Collinson's 1856 *The Siege of Sebastopol, by an Eye-witness* (Pl. 26), or Charles Hunt's 1870 *The Tribunal* (Pl. 22). Moreover, boys (unlike girls) are rarely shown as being contrite for their actions, probably because their decision making, for better or for worse, was deemed part of the prelude to manhood and thus required neither explanations nor apologies.

Not surprisingly, the Victorian notion of play was grounded in the prevailing expectations of each sex. The sexes were not always segregated in school (especially country schoolrooms) or during recreational activities, but when shown together, boys and girls usually maintain their assigned roles. Thus, girls were expected to be less troublesome because they were supposedly more spiritual; middle-class boys, on the other hand, could at least be more aggressive and self-directed than their dainty and rather boringly predictable sisters. It is interesting that both male and female artists put forth the same stereotypical viewpoints of childhood and the sexes, thus producing a fairly unified perspective of the period's cultural and ideological beliefs.

But what about the theme of the vagrant child or waif? This was another popular subject, yet as one historian has commented, the middle classes could in many senses afford the luxury of childhood, while the innocence of the lower classes was, by comparison, short-lived and endangered. One of the few artists who dealt with both classes—the Cockney slum child and the rich little heir or heiress—was John Leech, who spared neither group his acerbic pen in his cartoons for *Punch*. His upper-class children ape grown-up manners, dress, and bons mots, frequently acting like bratty and snobbish enfants terribles. Nor were his street urchins particularly sentimentalized and, typically, they affronted readers with their scruffy and irrepressibly cheeky behavior.

In truth, by mid-century the problem of the armies of neglected and destitute children in cities like London was a mounting one, and efforts were made by Mary Carpenter and others to cope with juvenile vice, crime, abuse, and homelessness. The city youngsters described in Henry Mayhew's classic 1861 tomes, *London Labour* and *The Labour Poor*, for example, seem to have had little chance to be children; instead they had to learn how to survive on the streets by selling firewood, matches, and the like. Public outcry about the need for labor laws, while sometimes vociferous, could not solve the problem of child workers, and for many years legislation failed to guarantee protection for those young employees who toiled in textile and other mill industries for as long as seventy-two hours a week. Furthermore, illiteracy was a national problem until the 1870 Education Act was passed.

While Dickens in his *Bleak House* of 1853 and other novels depicted the more wretched realities of half-savage street urchins who swore, stole, and lied, these sordid aspects of Victorian life were considerably glossed over in contemporary art. In William Powell Frith's 1881 *For Better, For Worse* (Pl. 19), for example, the ostensible subject derives from the title and the newlyweds' vows, but to modern viewers the underlying theme involves the ironic confrontation on the London streets of the "haves" and the "have-nots." The vagabond bands of urban children in Victorian art rarely seem threatening or malevolent, and the protagonists are neither criminals nor real victims, functioning instead mostly as creatures that allow the spectator a sympathetic or even a bemused response.

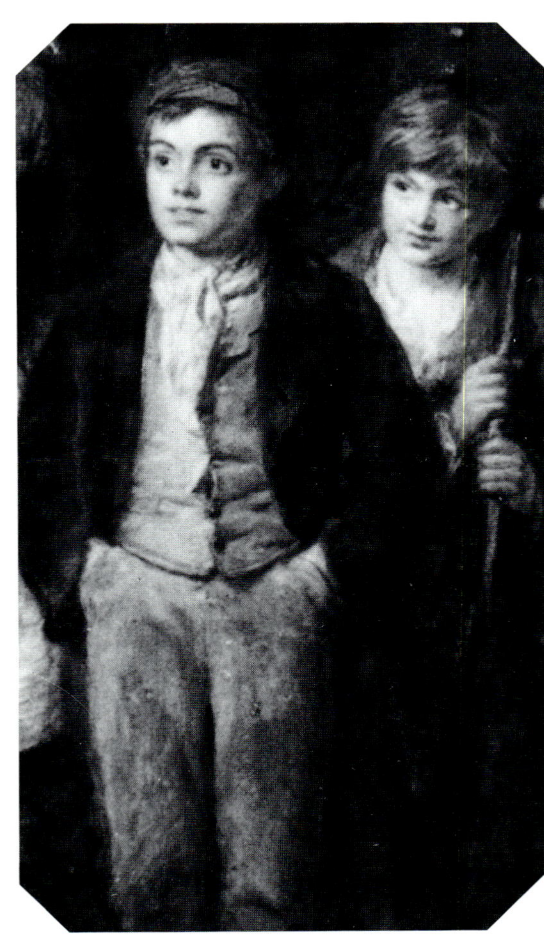

Detail from *For Better, For Worse*

It is thus no surprise that with the nostalgia for the past and the sentimentalizing of the present in the portrayal of childhood there were few hints in Victorian art of the oppressive sweatshops or mines that enslaved child laborers, of the horrifying "baby farms" where infants were kept while their parents worked, of sexually exploited child prostitutes, or even of troubled adolescents, although these problems existed and were mirrored in varying degrees in Victorian fiction. This avoidance of the painful elements of real life was one of many manifestations of displacement by the middle class, who by sublimating and replacing disturbing subjects with a more sanitized, safer version, could reduce life itself to simple child's play. (Nevertheless, toward the end of the century there were some modern and French-influenced artists like Whistler, Sargent, Steer, and members of the Newlyn School who often depicted children in a less sentimental light.)

The overall message of Victorian artists seems to be that children, whatever their class or sex, should display obedience, diligence, and acceptance of their lot—and that basically, boys should be aggressive and girls passive in preparation for their adult roles. The family, especially the middle-class one, is seen as a bastion of security and comfort, with relatively rare moments of serious dissension. Much scholarship remains to be done on the interrelationship between Victorian novels and paintings as well as on the greater realism of the literary form, for it is both curious and provocative that writers of the period less often tended to cosmeticize real life. Specific motifs like the boy sucking on a disciplinary rod seem distinctly Dickensian, and the latent layers of meaning of this image and of others—such as the girl holding a blossoming flower, the child juxtaposed with a pet, and the nursing infant—require more research and analysis.

Furthermore, questions must be asked about any subversive themes that surfaced as well as whether the typical picture of nostalgic and rather blissful rural childhood is actually closer to the truth than has been previously maintained. Whatever the direction of future hypotheses, the numbers and intensity of Victorian canvases treating the subject of children and childhood will probably continue to offer fascinating visual material as well as sometimes controversial interpretations of social history. This strand of imagery basically affirmed middle-class values of social benevolence and solidity, even in the face of increasing industrialization and other social woes. Yet beneath these messages may lurk a degree of covert fear of and resistance to any real changes in the status quo.

Society sanctioned the Victorian veneration and rediscovery of childhood in art and allowed adults to experience again or re-awaken memories of their own or their children's youth in ways that were not fully understood in pre-Freudian times. And while there is undoubtedly an element of escapism and wishful thinking in such narrative pictures, there is also a lot to be learned. Perhaps it is a nearly universal adult need in Western cultures to preserve and promote a myth of childhood in predominantly rosy terms, in order to satisfy the need for emotional continuity between art and life and to enable people to cope with the joys and sorrows of the past and the present.

S.P.C.

# VICTORIAN CHILDHOOD

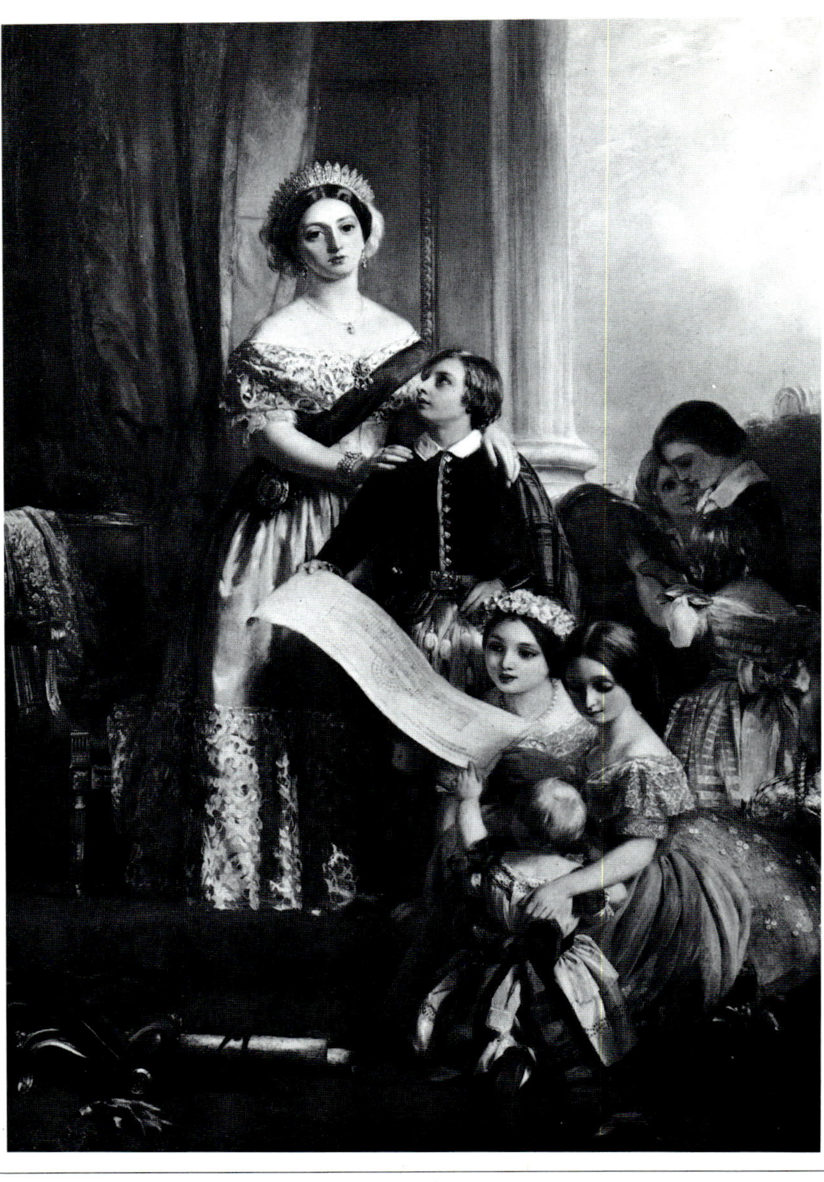

Plate 1

JOHN CALLCOTT HORSLEY (1817–1903)

*A PORTRAIT GROUP OF QUEEN VICTORIA WITH HER CHILDREN*, ca. 1865

Oil on canvas, 47 × 33″

The nephew of a well-known artist, John Horsley entered the Royal Academy schools at the age of fourteen and later won praise for his murals in the House of Lords and the House of Parliament. His *Rent Day at Haddon Hall in the Days of Queen Elizabeth*, 1839, established the standard for numerous subsequent costume pieces set in earlier historical periods, often on the grounds of Haddon Hall or other eminent Elizabethan or Jacobean estates. Until 1896 Horsley also exhibited many genre pictures and literary illustrations at the Academy, including such titles as *Malvolio i' the sun*, 1849, *Milton Dictating Samson Agonistes*, 1859, *The Bashful Swain*, 1864, and *Madame Se Chauffe* of 1871.

A larger version of this portrait of the royal family was exhibited in 1865, four years after the death of the Queen's beloved Prince Albert. Many artists—including Edwin Landseer and Franz Winterhalter—produced portraits of Queen Victoria, but this one has a curiously poignant quality to it. In their life together the royal couple symbolized Victorian domesticity and harmony at the nation's helm; even without the Prince, Victoria reigns over both her family and the nation. Here she is shown standing pensively amid a cluster of seven of their nine offspring, who are amusing one another. The future King Edward VII (who wears a tartan, a fashion Queen Victoria much admired) looks up rather seriously at his mother; he has obviously been examining the blueprint plans of his father's great project, the Crystal Palace, which is also alluded to by the building in the background right.

Horsley wrote in his *Recollections* of a portrait of the infant Princess Beatrice commissioned by the Queen in 1858 as a gift for Prince Albert, but he makes no mention of when this group family portrait was painted. If it was executed after the Prince Consort's death, then the pointedly empty chair at the monarch's right can be interpreted as an allusion to his death. His son now occupies his place by the Queen's side. Prince Albert's achievements in the Great Exhibition of 1851 are also balanced against the personal legacy of a large brood of children which he has left to be raised by his grieving widow. In the face of the death of the paterfamilias, the plight of his offspring and widowed Victoria probably personified to many contemporary viewers the nobility and endurance of the Victorian middle-class family.

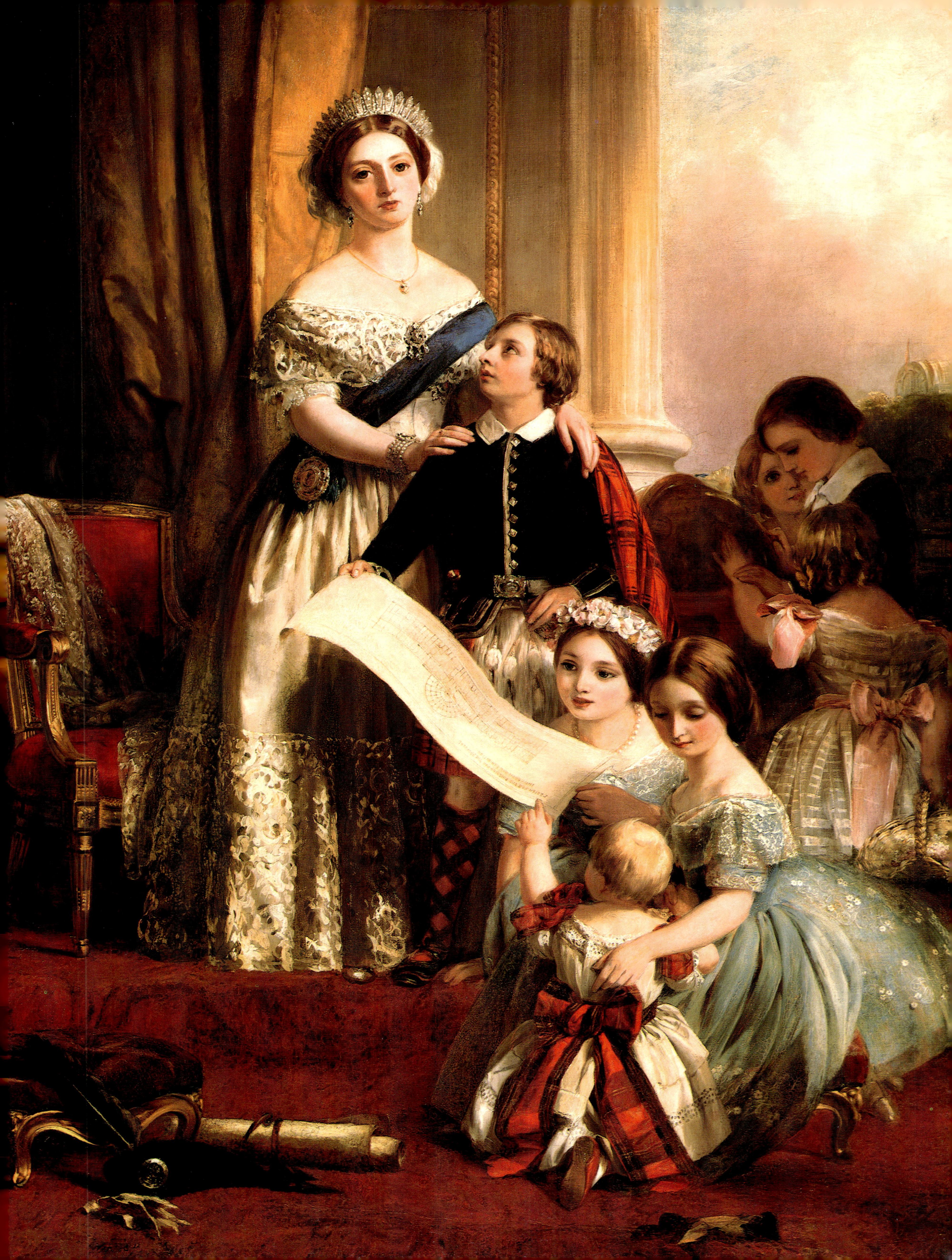

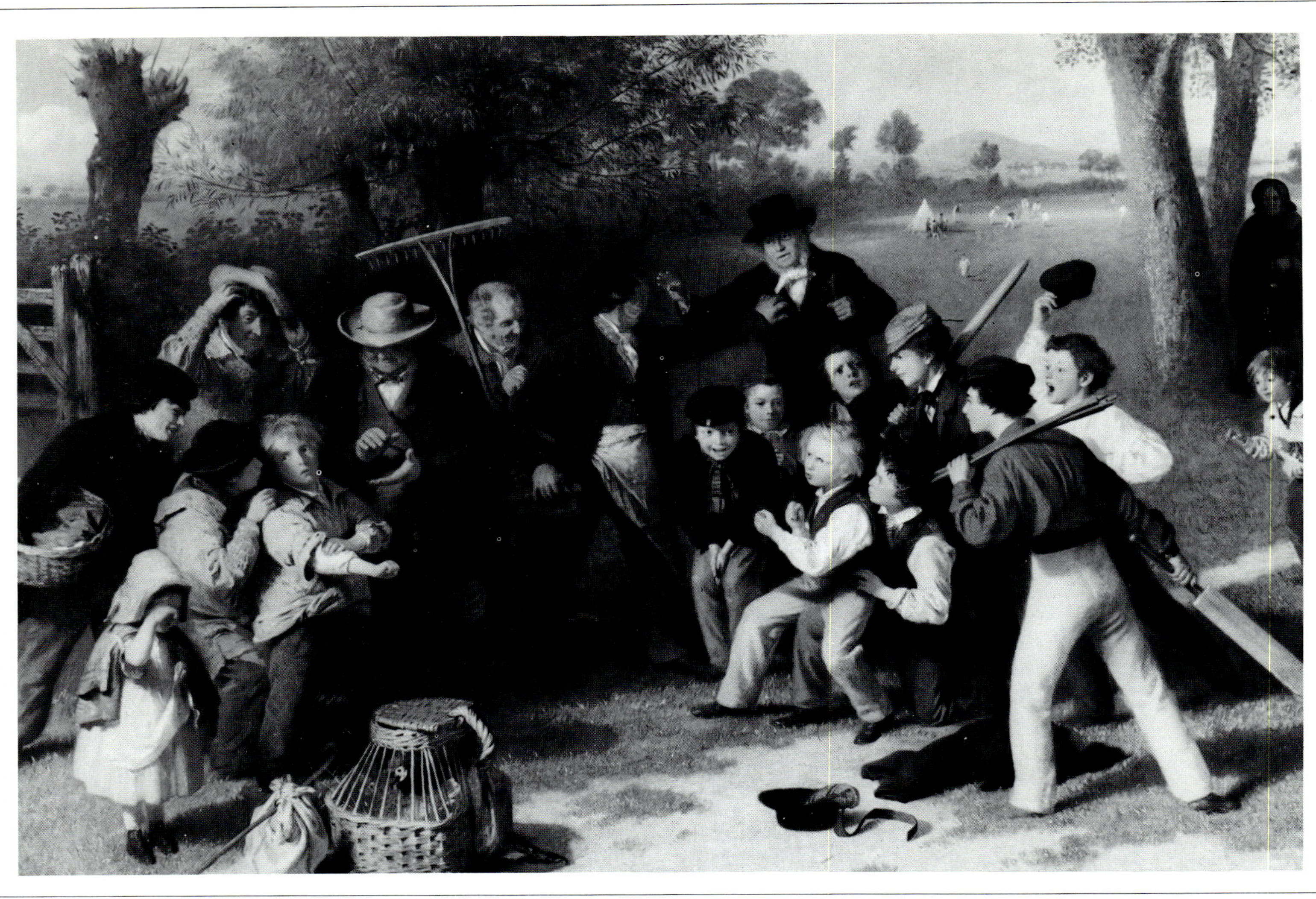

Plate 2

JOHN MORGAN (1823–1886)

*THE FIGHT*, 1869

Oil on canvas, 26 × 40″

John Morgan exhibited over one hundred paintings at the Society of British Artists between 1853–86 as well as a great many others during the same period at the Royal Academy and the British Institution. While some of his subjects were literary and historical, many had titles like *Mischief*, 1855, *The Playfellows*, 1857, *Goodnight, Mamma*, 1864, *Snowballing*, 1865, and *Left at School*, 1871–2, and they clearly reflect the artist's interest in the theme of childhood.

When *The Fight* was exhibited at the Royal Academy in 1869 it was hailed by *The Art Journal* as "perhaps the cleverest genre picture in this gallery, if not in the whole Academy." This scene of "schoolboy quarrel and tussel . . . has made itself a favorite among exhibition-goers," and the picture was also deemed worthy of Thomas Webster, a Victorian master of this type of painting. In public schools a variety of team games were played, and one of the most popular—cricket—is visible in the background right. English football was also a rather ferocious sport, especially before the reforms enacted to tame its violence. Not surprisingly, the playing fields were, in real life as in Victorian fiction, the place where boys tested their masculinity and prowess, with bullies often seizing upon younger or smaller lads as suitable targets or prey.

In *The Fight* the antagonists seem to come from two different classes, the country boy at left rolling up his sleeves and being urged on by his rustic mates while his opponent at right is being similarly exhorted by his schoolboy colleagues. (One may assume that the country boys are probably uneducated, since the Education Act affecting the lower classes in particular was not established until the year after this painting was completed.) The older spectators also cheer on their favorites, and an incipient disagreement between the rustic fellow with the apron and basket and the squire behind him parallels the belligerence of the youthful males. While the adult males carry potentially threatening weapons—one a rake, the other a cane—some of the middle-class boys grip cricket bats and other sports equipment capable of bludgeoning an opponent. Between the two warring groups there is a space where the fistfight will take place and to the left a caged rooster that evokes the thought of gory cockfights. Significantly, while the males of all ages and classes seem to relish this opportunity for a skirmish, the only females are distressed observers—both the weeping little country lass at lower left and the older woman—possibly the squire's wife—glumly watching beneath a tree in the mid-ground right. While sometimes the sexes may have shared the same territory and values, here the segregation of roles and spheres is quite distinct.

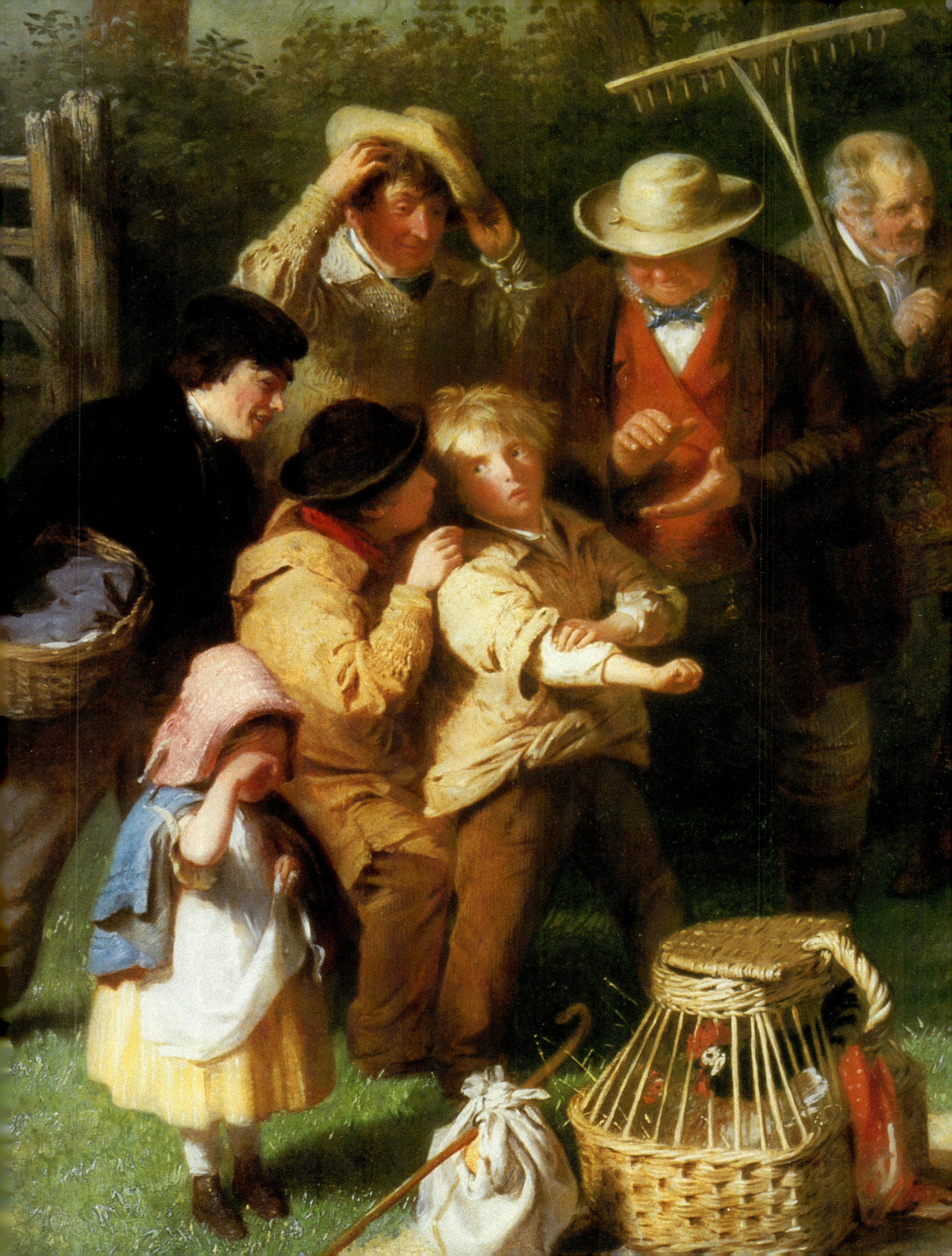

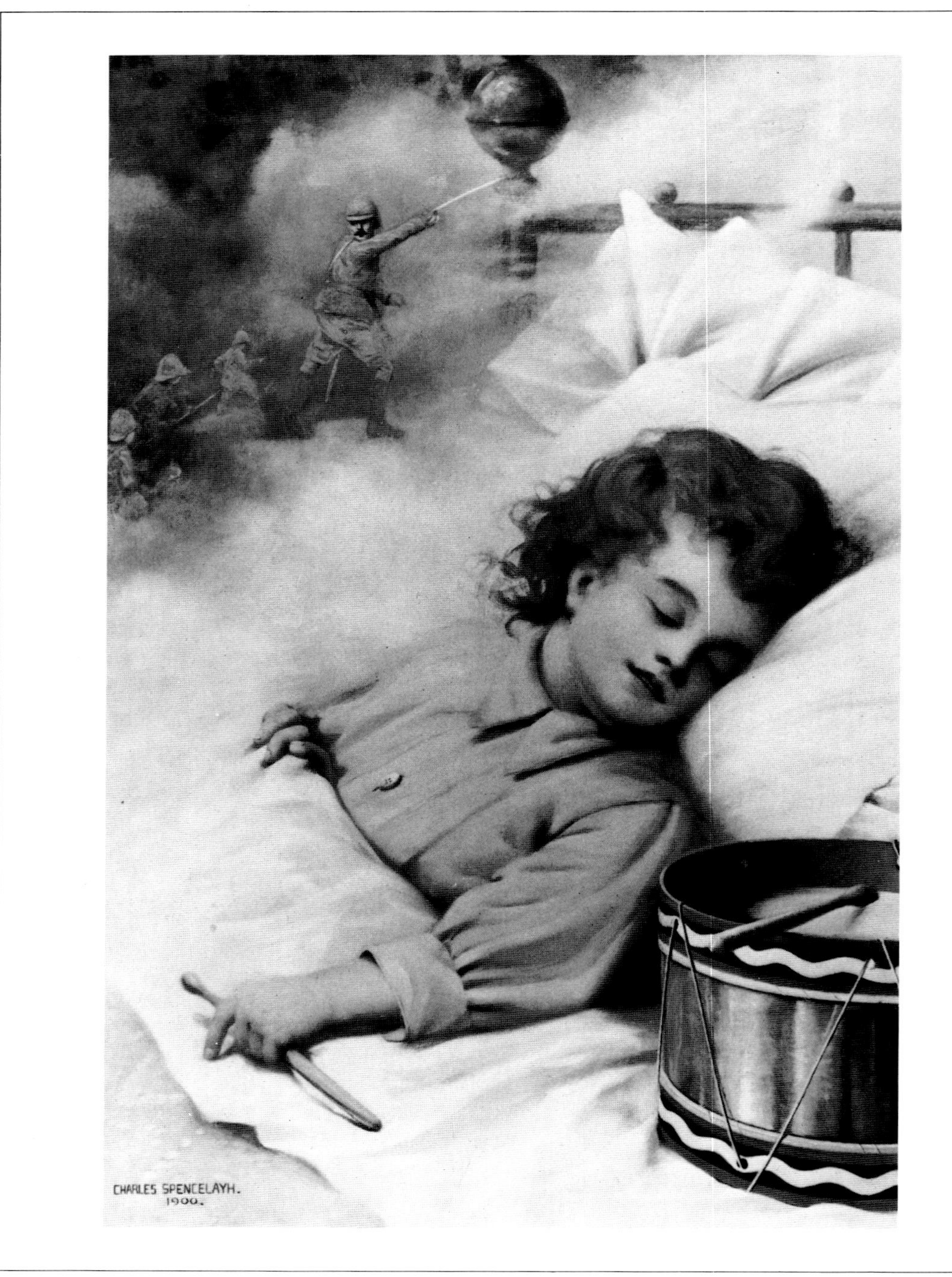


Plate 3

CHARLES SPENCELAYH (1866–1958)

*DREAMS OF GLORY*, 1900

Oil on canvas, 30 × 20″

After studying at the Kensington School of Art, Charles Spencelayh became a portrait and figure painter whose versatility encompassed etchings and miniatures. Many of his works were exhibited at the Royal Society of Artists, Birmingham, the Royal Miniature Society, the Royal Institute of Oil Painters, and the Royal Academy. His long career spanned more than half a century of stylistic changes in English art, and his subject matter often reflected the realities of war or personal struggle. He continued exhibiting until the end of his life, in the 1940s producing works concerned with World War II, bearing titles such as *Dig for Victory*, *More Coupons*, and *Winning the War*.

*Dreams of Glory* was painted around the time of the Boer War (1899–1902), and perhaps that military campaign influenced the artist's choice of subject. In addition to war-related themes, several of Spencelayh's works concentrate on the relationship between generations, often picturing a grandparent and grandchild. In this painting the sole subject is a sleeping boy, a "little soldier" who presumably dreams of victory and the glamour and excitement of combat. In one hand he holds a drumstick, while near the pillow lies a drum of the sort that young drummer boys beat for the troops marching off to battle.

The child's fantasies have materialized above his head in a group of soldiers with guns, and it has been suggested that the round bedstead finial looks like a small globe or world, perhaps symbolizing the global strength of the British Empire in military as well as other matters. Typically, in Spencelayh's canvases we see faithfully transcribed rooms, but in *Dreams of Glory* the setting is a close-up view of a bed and its occupant rather than a complete bedroom interior.

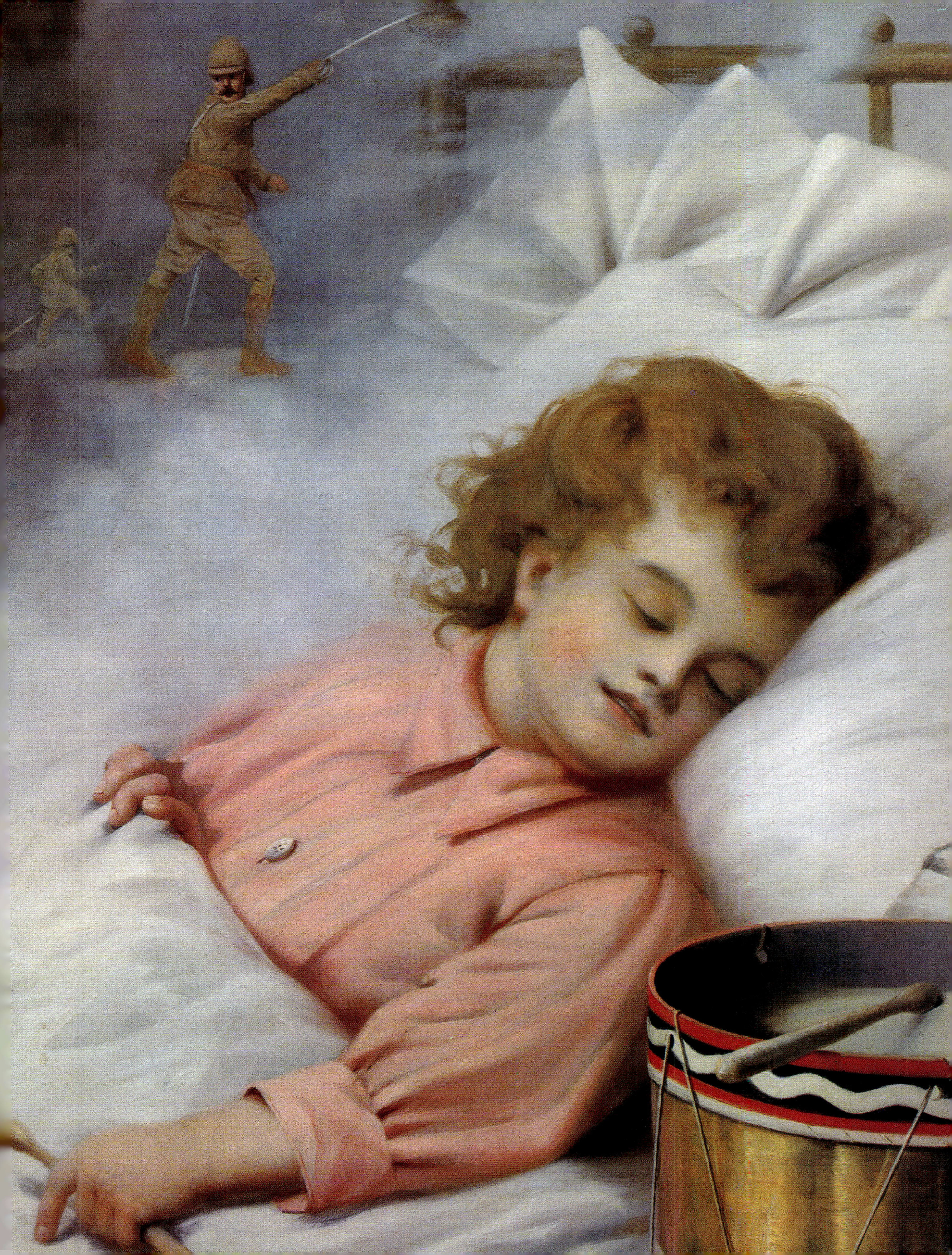

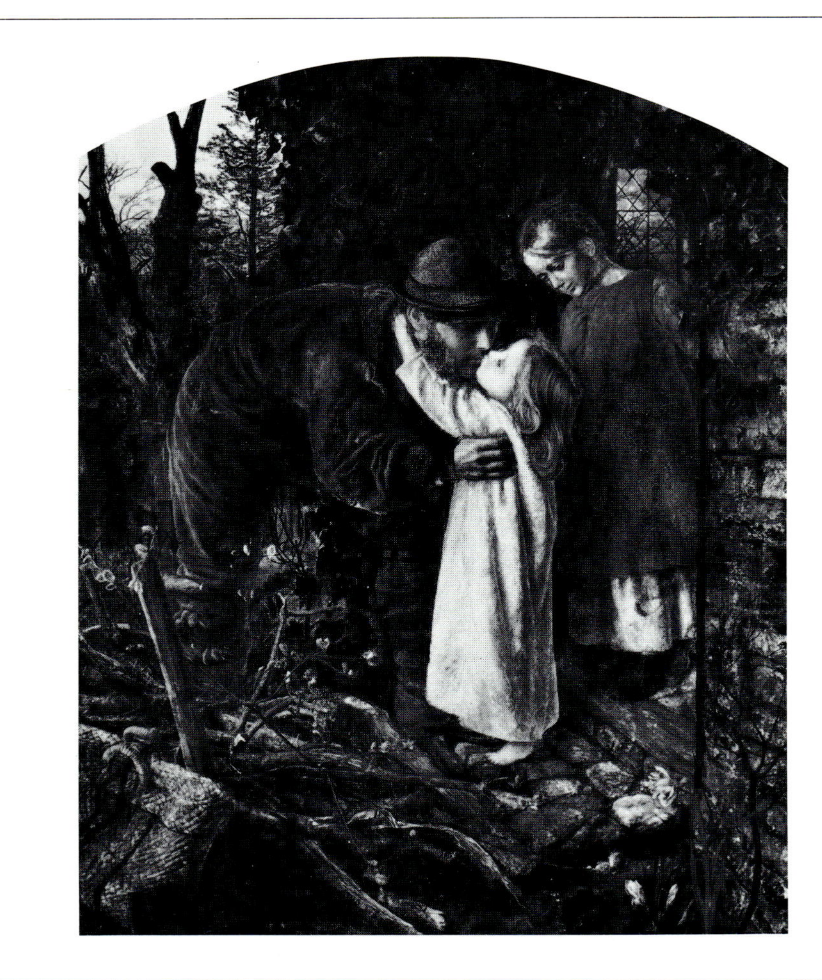

Plate 4

ARTHUR HUGHES (1832–1915)

*HOME FROM WORK*, 1861

Oil on canvas (arched top), 40½ × 31

After a few years of study at the Royal Academy, Arthur Hughes converted to Pre-Raphaelitism, supposedly after reading the magazine, *The Germ*, and he became a friend of most of the members of the Brotherhood, especially of John Everett Millais. Apparently a rather pious and gentle man, Hughes was often the butt of good-natured jokes from his friends, who nonetheless made him an unofficial part of their circle; after 1855 he retired to a quiet life outside London where he continued to produce paintings and book illustrations.

Hughes's first Pre-Raphaelite canvas was *Ophelia*, exhibited in 1847, and within a few years his own style of microscopic detail, poetic intensity, and luminous color developed. Many of his canvases are densely packed, almost claustrophobic spaces filled with pattern and foliage, but in *Home From Work* (the artist's sole Royal Academy entry of 1861), this effect is softened somewhat by a glowing sunset sky in the distance. The painting represents a woodsman's return home at the end of the day, to be met by his two daughters, one a beautiful young child in a white nightgown who throws her arms around the man's neck and stands on tip-toe for a kiss. Although *The Athenaeum* thought the picture "somewhat over-coloured in the half-tints," thus generating a somewhat stained-glass effect, it applauded the loving expression and pronounced the infant "quite kissable." *The Art Journal* praised the canvas as "one of the most intense and one of the best specimens of Pre-Raphaelism" in the exhibition that year, commenting favorably on both the carefully painted detail and the tender emotion shared by the father and child. The critic complained, however, that the figures could have been made more attractive and decried "this rage for ugliness and stiffness," for the Pre-Raphaelite creed of meticulous fidelity to nature or anatomy often resulted in visual effects (especially in portraiture) that were quite extraordinary and unsettling. Hughes also produced a few other paintings that enshrined the peace and value of the home, including an 1862 work entitled *Bed Time*, in which his own wife and children appear as the happy subjects.

Both the arched top and the ivy-covered wall owe an obvious debt to Millais's masterpiece, *A Huguenot*, 1852, and there may also be parallels of pose and character intended with Millais's *The Rescue*, 1855, as well as with *Autumn Leaves*, 1856. The elder sister at the doorway was described by *The Athenaeum* as "a sweet English child of twelve, rosy with health and fair, with good Saxon blood . . . half proud with sympathy, half patronizingly, and pleasantly loving in her happiness." A surrogate mother, she watches as a younger sibling rushes to welcome their father; some of the foliage outside the cottage is symbolic, in the Victorian language of flowers, of innocence and regeneration. As the child holds on to her father, so too does the ivy cling to its support, both emblems in different ways of constancy or faithfulness. The delicate purity and angelic appearance of the child is contrasted with the work-worn and dirty face of the parent, who has left behind a day of toil to be received at the gates of his own private paradise, his humble home.

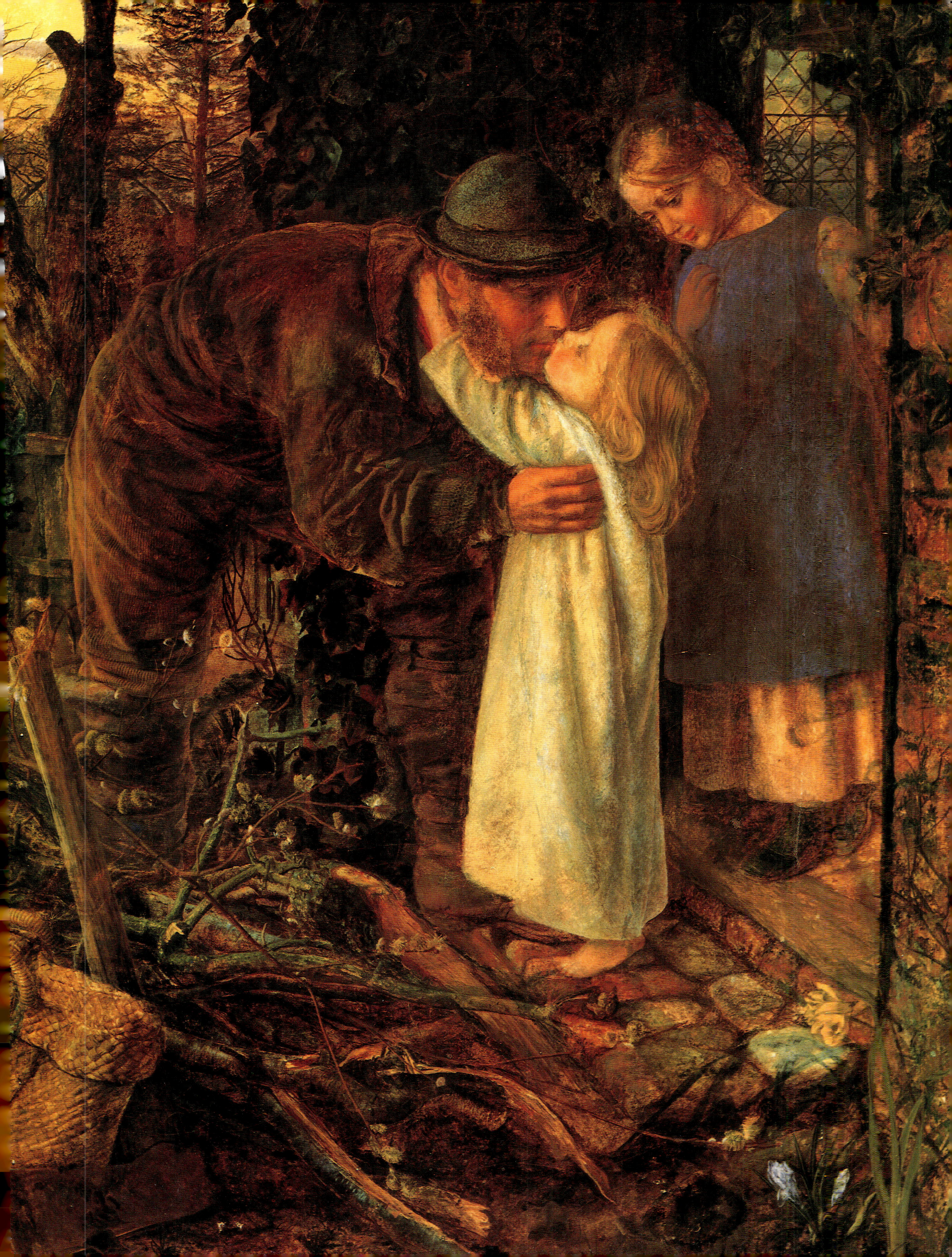

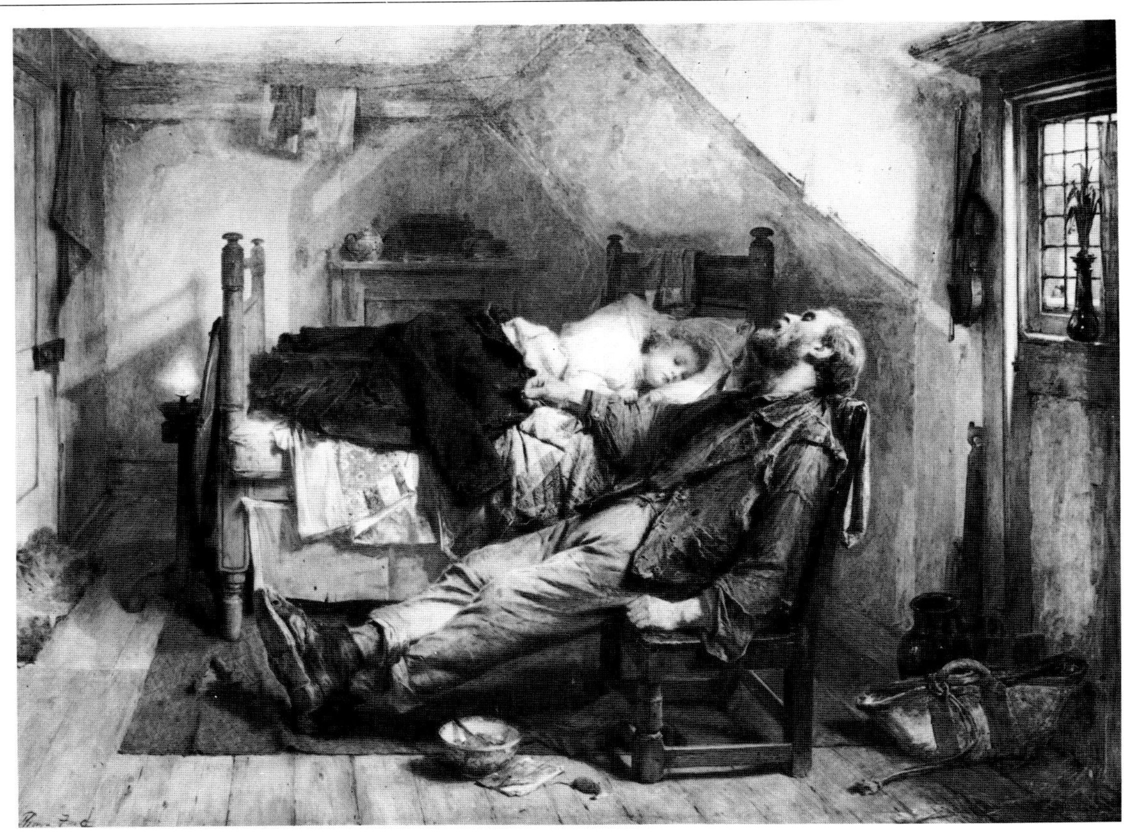

Plate 5

THOMAS FAED (1826–1900)

*WORN OUT*, 1868

Oil on canvas, 41¾ × 57″

Thomas Faed, another child prodigy, followed his elder brother John into an artistic career after joining him in Edinburgh in 1843. The younger brother was very successful as an art student, winning several prizes for his scenes of rural Scottish life or literary subjects, and gaining patronage from collectors such as Henry Wallis in London. By the age of 23 he had already exhibited nearly two dozen paintings at the Royal Scottish Academy and he began contributing to London's Royal Academy in 1851, continuing until 1893. In 1852 he moved to London (where his brother would later join him), in time selling his canvases for high prices to important dealers such as Thomas Agnew and Sons, Louis Flatow, and Ernest Gambart. Faed's most productive decade was 1860 to 1870, and he enjoyed a retrospective exhibition of his work in 1860 staged by Agnew's, a rare homage for a living artist. Faed thus enjoyed both popularity with the public and a good reputation among the critics, a winning combination for any painter.

By 1868 when *Worn Out* was exhibited at the Royal Academy, Faed had scored numerous successes in the art world, notably his *The Mitherless Bairn*, 1855, and its pendant *Home and the Homeless* of the following year, as well as his "emigration pictures" such as *The First Break in the Family*, 1857, *Sunday in the Backwoods*, 1859, and *The Last of the Clan*, 1865. All of these paintings had subjects that were poignant, even tear-jerking, and this is also true of *Worn Out*, where the exhausted father and the sick child give us a hint of working-class fatalism about illness and death. *The Art Journal* pronounced the work impressive, adding "yet another chapter to his pathetic annals of the poor. . . . The story is told with a circumstantial detail which comes home to the heart. . . . The harmony of his broken tones, the texture of his surfaces, are in keeping with the class of subjects to which he is devoted." So powerful was the effect of this picture that the Archbishop of York mentioned it at the annual Royal Academy banquet, noting that "the contemplation of such works . . . which show us human nature in moments of defeat and distress, is very good for all social classes to appreciate." The painting became quite well known and one lower-class spectator commented, when *Worn Out* was displayed in 1890, that the theme revealed that "it's not always the clothes that show the heart, is it?"

In fact, Faed often painted vignettes that emphasized paternal affection and solicitude for children, to some extent countering the impression of upper-class remoteness, and stereotypes about lower-class or rural harshness towards the family. (He also produced a few scenes of maternal solicitude, including sickbed scenes such as *Mother's First Care*, 1873, and *The Doctor's Visit*.)

Here, however, a working-class man, perhaps a carpenter from the evidence of the tools in the room, has tended his ill little son all through a long and restless night. Both are now "worn out" as dawn breaks, but it is not clear whether the battle with illness has been won or the child will succumb. The motherless boy still holds on to his father's sleeve, a detail that movingly reinforces the bond existing between father and son. The parent has obviously taken great pains to care for and please the young invalid, for there is a tattered book dropped on the floor, a violin on the wall for entertaining him, and a mat placed against the door to keep out cold drafts. *The Athenaeum* critic also speculated that the father had laid his best coat over his child for warmth and that "the candle is shown placed behind the foot-board, so that . . . its light is shaded from the sufferer's eyes." What little they have to eat is being shared on the floor by a mouse that snatches a crumb of food. The pot of flowers on the windowsill is a constant reminder in genre pictures of the state of the occupants' health as well as a touch of nature in contrast to the grim urban setting.

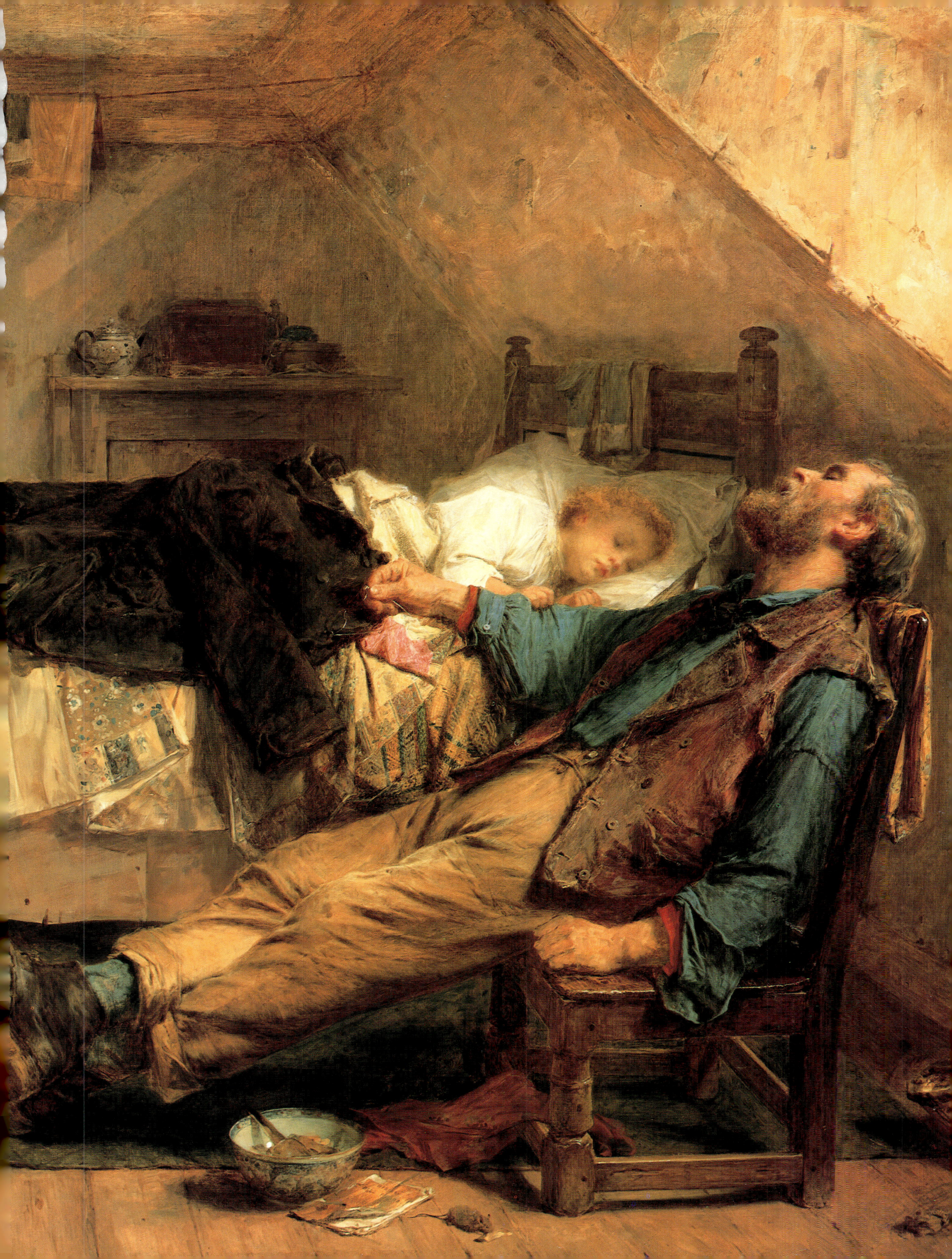

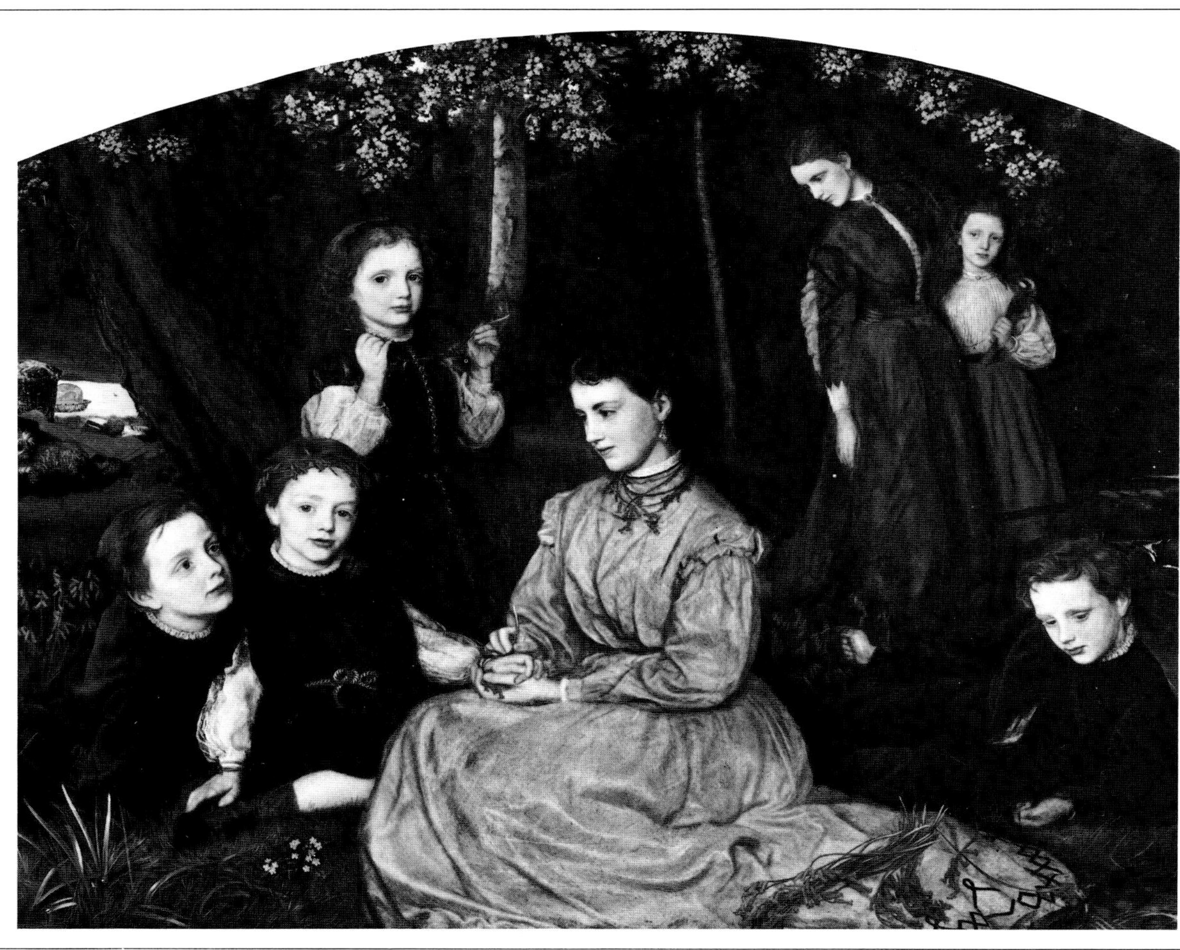

Plate 6

ARTHUR HUGHES (1832–1915)

*A BIRTHDAY PICNIC*, 1867

Oil on canvas, 39 × 50″

One of the more important figures in the Pre-Raphaelite circle (although only proposed as a member of the Brotherhood), Arthur Hughes painted canvases that generally bore the direct imprint of Pre-Raphaelite style; some of his colors—especially his lyrical hues of purple—were quite idiosyncratic. By 1856 his *April Love* was a full-blown exercise in Pre-Raphaelitism, and this style continued in other subject pictures such as *Home from Work*, 1861, *Home from Sea*, 1863, and *Silver and Gold*, 1864.

While he continued to paint some genre and literary pictures for the Royal Academy in the 1860s until 1902, Hughes also illustrated children's books, and he produced a number of portraits as well. In 1865 he exhibited a painting of *Mrs. James Leathart and Children*, the family of an eminent patron of the arts, and in 1879 he produced a final commission in which eleven children stand, sit, listen, or play musical instruments. In the same decade, Hughes also painted the portraits of the family of Thomas Brighton, a self-made man of wealth not unlike Leathart who was a major industrialist in Newcastle. In another commissioned group portrait, *A Birthday Picnic* (which was included in the Royal Academy of 1867), the results are equally charming. The sitters are the children of William and Anne Pattison of Felling, near Gateshead, and the picture's title commemorates the fifth birthday of Norman Perry Pattison, the second child from the left. The setting is a glen in Fellingwood, Northumberland, with in the background a picnic hamper, blanket, pile of hats, and family dog all awaiting attention. From left to right the children are: Hugh, Norman, Ethel, Victoria, Margaret, Edith Anne, and Walter. Hughes has tried to make this Victorian outdoor "conversation piece" as natural and naturalistic as possible; part of the underlying purpose of the gathering (aside from the birthday party) is the picking of flowers for adornment.

Young Norman wears a victor's wreath on his head, and his older sister (named after the Queen) wears a necklace of flowers. In a rather motherly way she takes the boy's hand and winds still more flowers around his wrist. Another sister is about to bend a branch of blossoms into a circlet, while somewhat apart, an older and younger sister stand in graceful embrace against the background of green woods. It is not clear whether the flowers themselves were chosen by the artist for any symbolic meaning, but this is a distinct possibility given the popularity of the "language of the flowers" in this period. A third brother lounges on the ground at right, his attitude quite beautifully casual. Other rather elegiac treatments of small groups of children or females in verdant settings can be found in James Archer's *Summertime, Gloucestershire* and John Everett Millais's *Apple Blossoms (Spring)*, 1856–9, for example, but this group portrait by Hughes generates a particularly tender and lyrical quality of family unity and bliss.

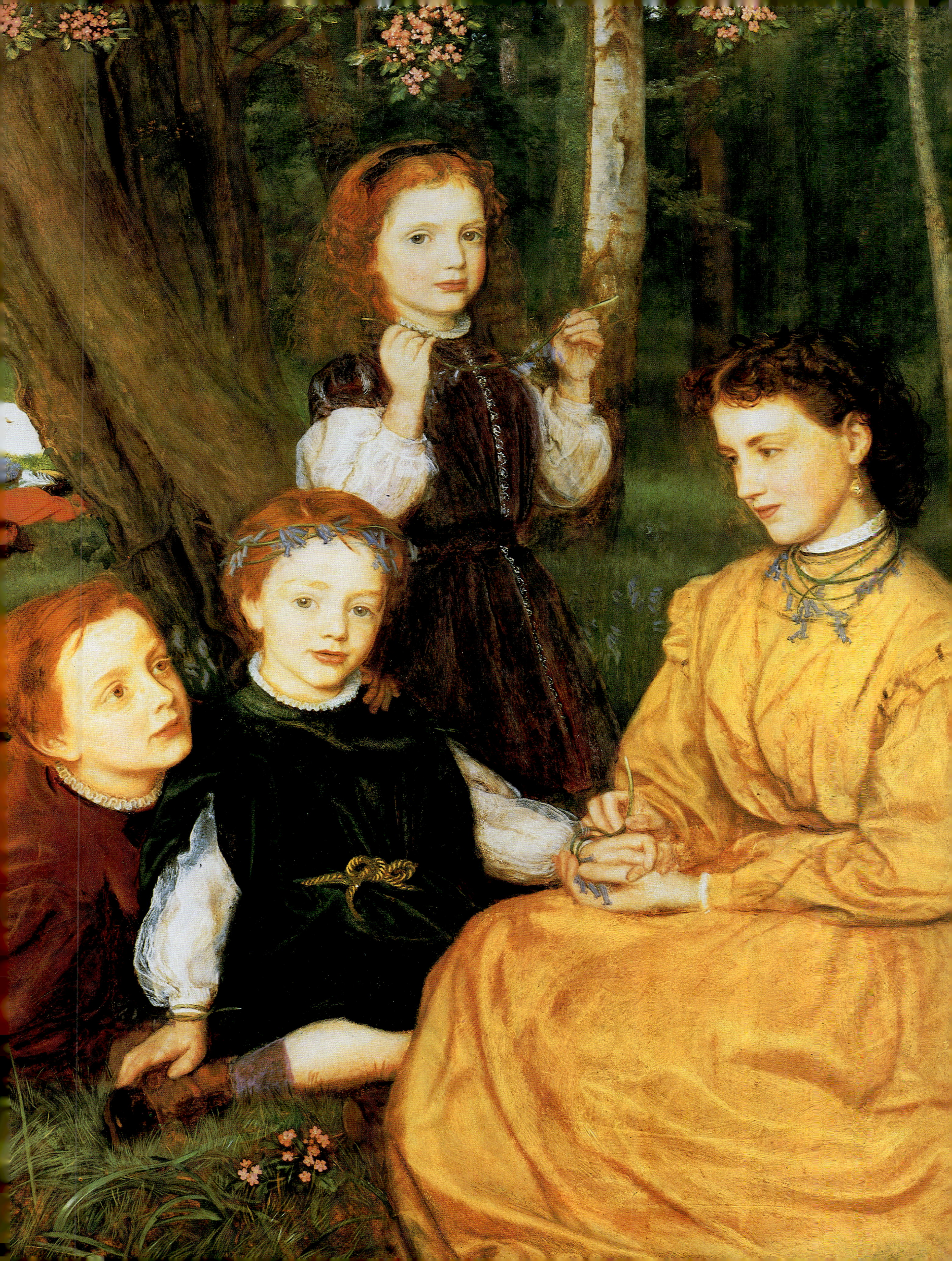

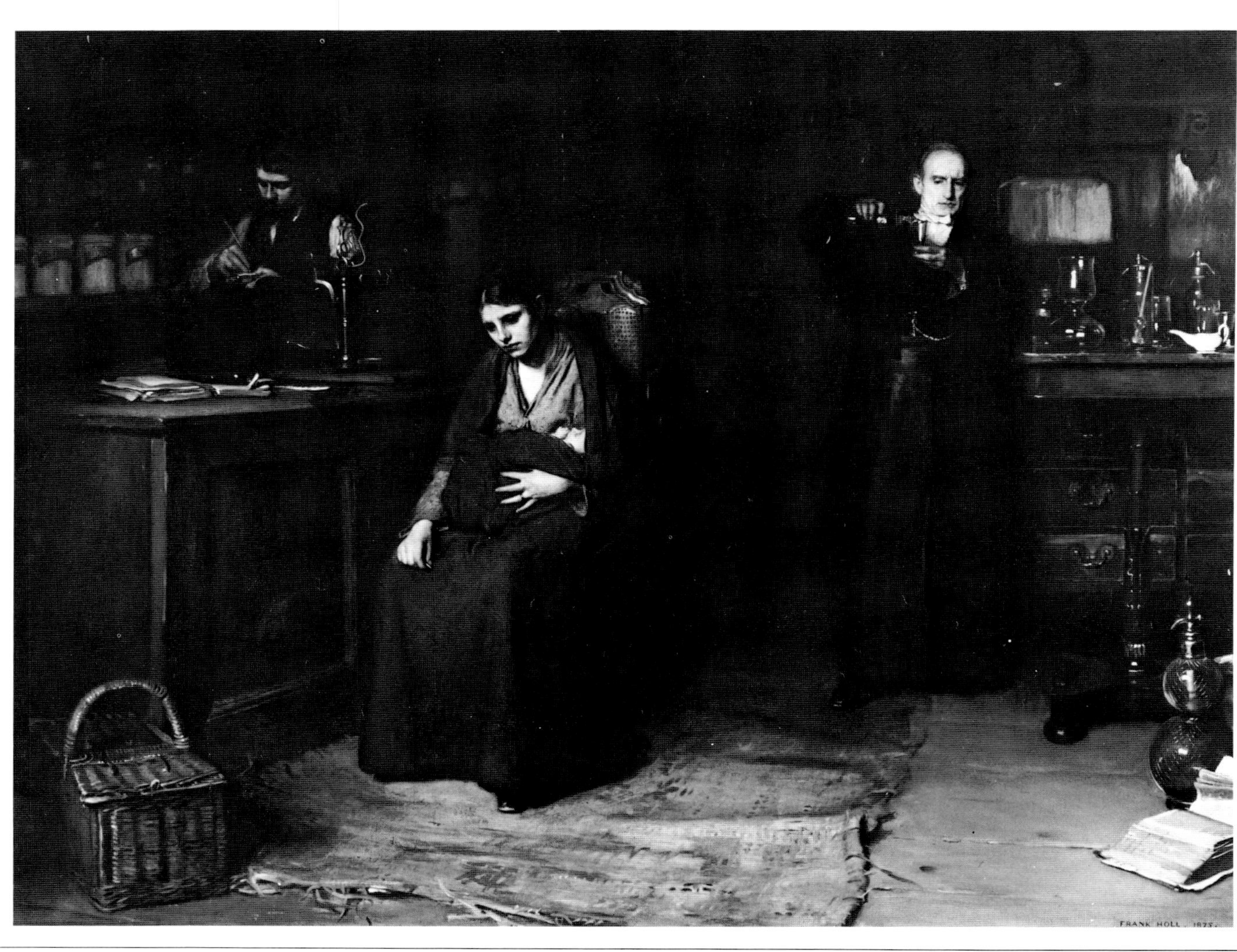

Plate 7

FRANK HOLL (1845–1888)

*DOUBTFUL HOPE*, 1875

Oil on canvas, 37½ × 53½″

In about 1870, Frank Holl and artists such as Luke Fildes and Hubert von Herkomer began to produce paintings with a strong vein of social realism that concentrated on the subject of rural and, more especially, urban poverty in England. Holl was only fifteen when he began his studies at the Royal Academy schools, and among his earliest exhibited works was *Turned out of Church*, 1864, with its subject of a beggar woman protecting her child during a rainstorm. Like Herkomer, Holl was hired in the early 1870s to produce illustrations for *The Graphic*, and these images also brought his brand of rather stark and depressing subject matter to the attention of the public.

*Doubtful Hope* is one of several pictures of the 1870s that are linked by their focus on the fate of the destitute or grieving woman and her child. Works in this category include *Want—Her Poverty but not Her Will Consents*, 1873, *Deserted—A Foundling*, 1874, and *Her First Born*, 1876. Holl was, in fact, often criticized for his gloomy and even morbid topics, and another lugubrious narrative is found in this canvas. Inside an apothecary shop, a dejected young mother with a babe in arms holds a coin and stares blankly at the floor as she waits for medicine for the dying child. Given the high infant mortality rate, such scenes were, in actuality, commonplace. As a reviewer pointed out in 1876, even the mother seems ill, and the pathos of gestures and facial expressions of all the figures conveys considerable emotional power.

The darkened interior here and in kindred pictures adds to the drama, and from this dusky atmosphere emerge the handsomely painted still-life elements of the glass apothecary bottles, the open book, the ragged basket, and the scale. Such scenes of poverty did occur in real life, and Holl's compassionate reporting of them gained him both admirers and critics.

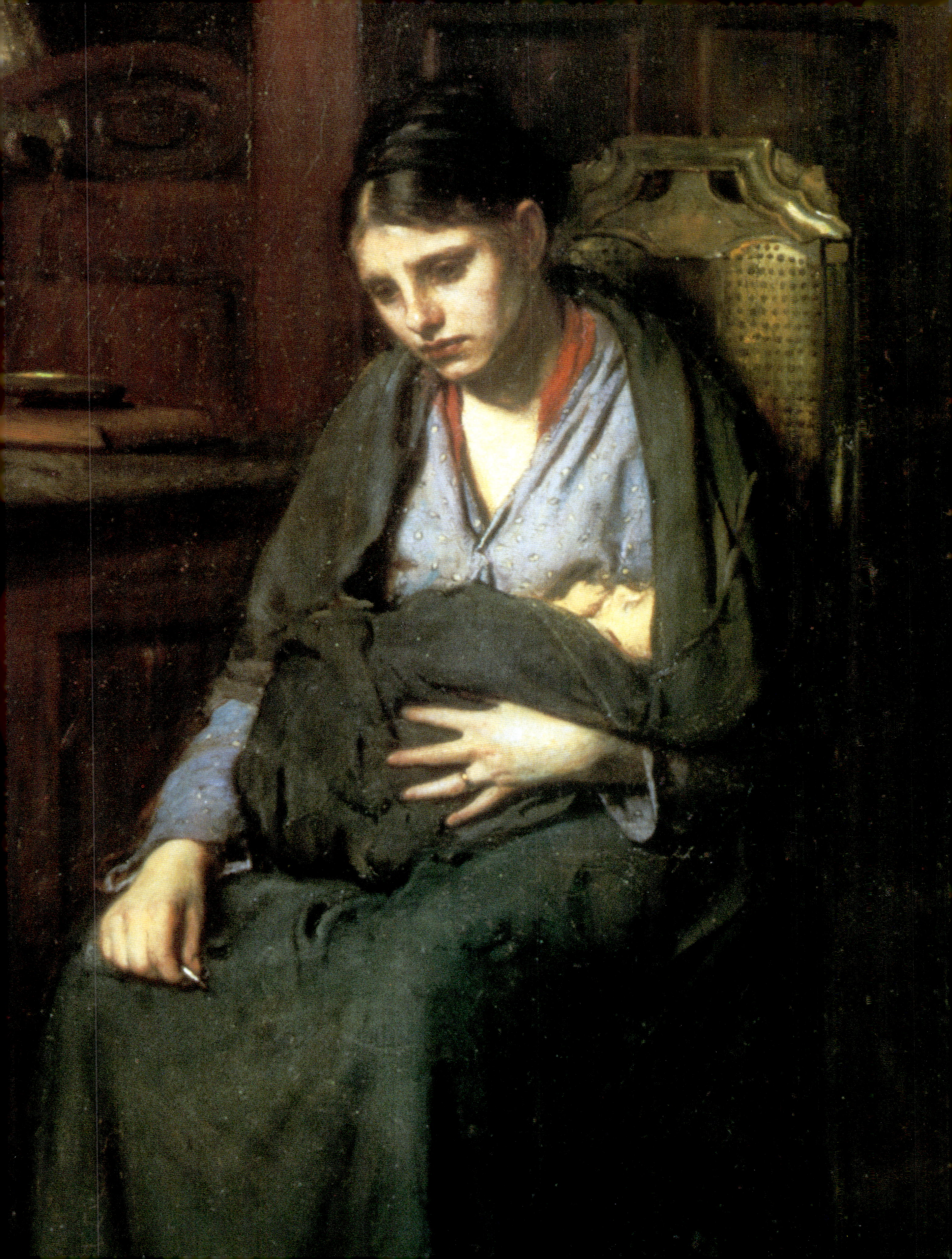

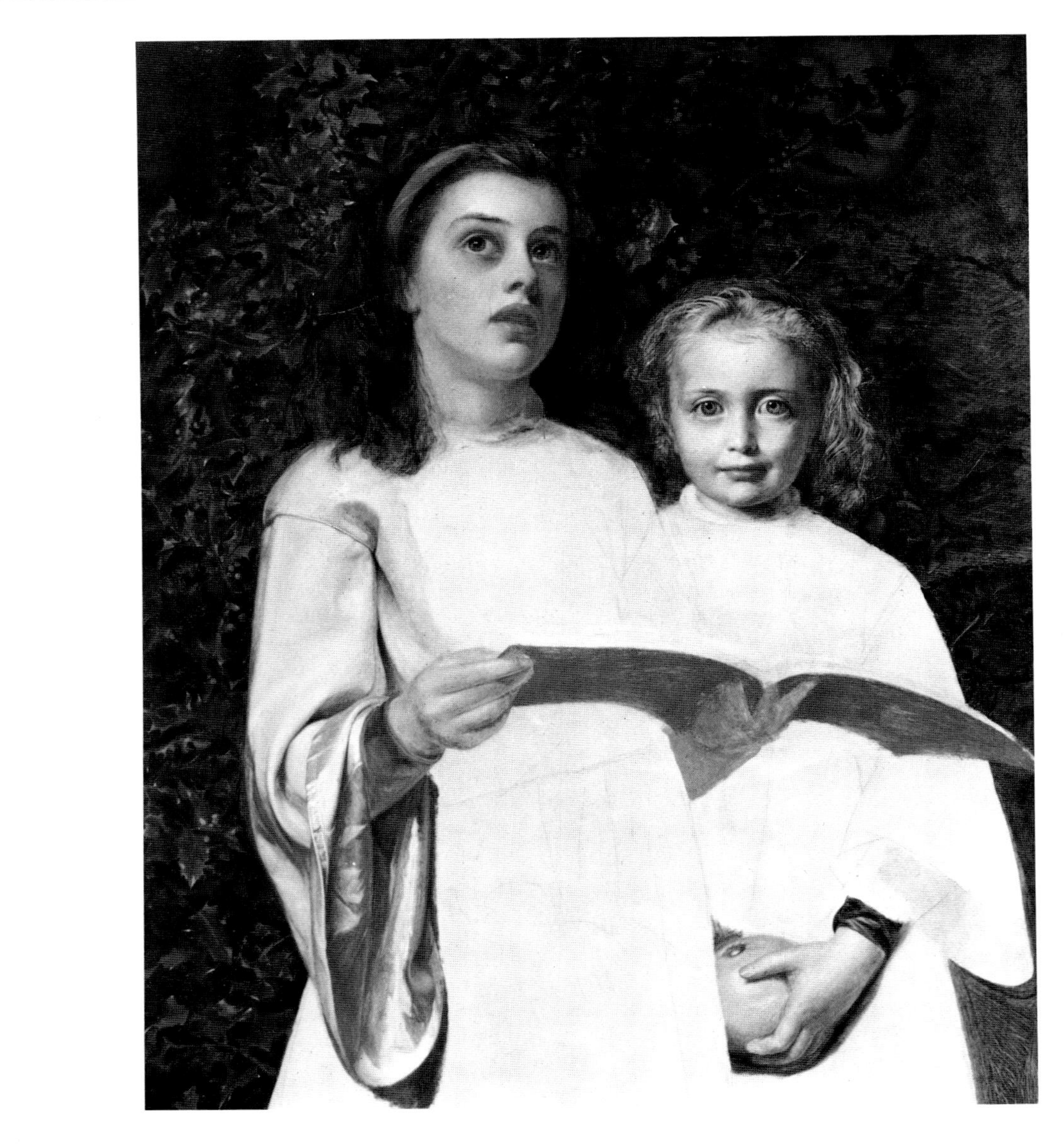

Plate 8

FREDERICK SANDYS (1829–1904)

*AT VESPERS*, ca. 1860

Oil on panel, 23½ × 19½″

Frederick Sandys began his professional career as a portraitist, exhibiting, for the most part, works of portraiture at the Royal Academy between 1851 and 1886. However, it was his 1857 caricature lampooning John Everett Millais's *Sir Isumbras at the Ford* that earned his entrée into the Pre-Raphaelite circle. There he became friendly with Dante Gabriel Rossetti in particular, sharing a house with him at Cheyne Walk. Rossetti later described his rather bohemian colleague as "the most brilliant of living draughtsmen," and it is as an illustrator and engraver that he made his reputation in the pages of *The Cornhill Magazine*, *Once a Week*, and other periodicals.

In the 1860s Sandys produced several magnificent portraits, among them female subjects such as *Mrs. Susannah Rose*, 1863, and *Mrs. Jane Lewis*, 1864. Later, he would move on to Rossettian icons of femininity and even portrayals of female evil and malevolence in such paintings as *Vivien*, 1863, and *Medea*, completed in 1868. After 1869 he almost totally abandoned the oil medium in order to work in colored chalk, and scores of provocative portraits of single figures (usually female) survive from this later period. The two young girls in *At Vespers* appear also in a chalk drawing by Sandys, but in this unfinished oil composition their faces have been idealized somewhat. One of this angelic pair holds an orange and the other a hymnal, and it is possible that the two lovely children were the artist's own daughters.

The foliate "screen" in the background is reminiscent of Rossetti's elaborately patterned niches for female figures, but there is no hint here of the malignant threat viewers perceive in many of Sandys's subsequent images of temptresses.

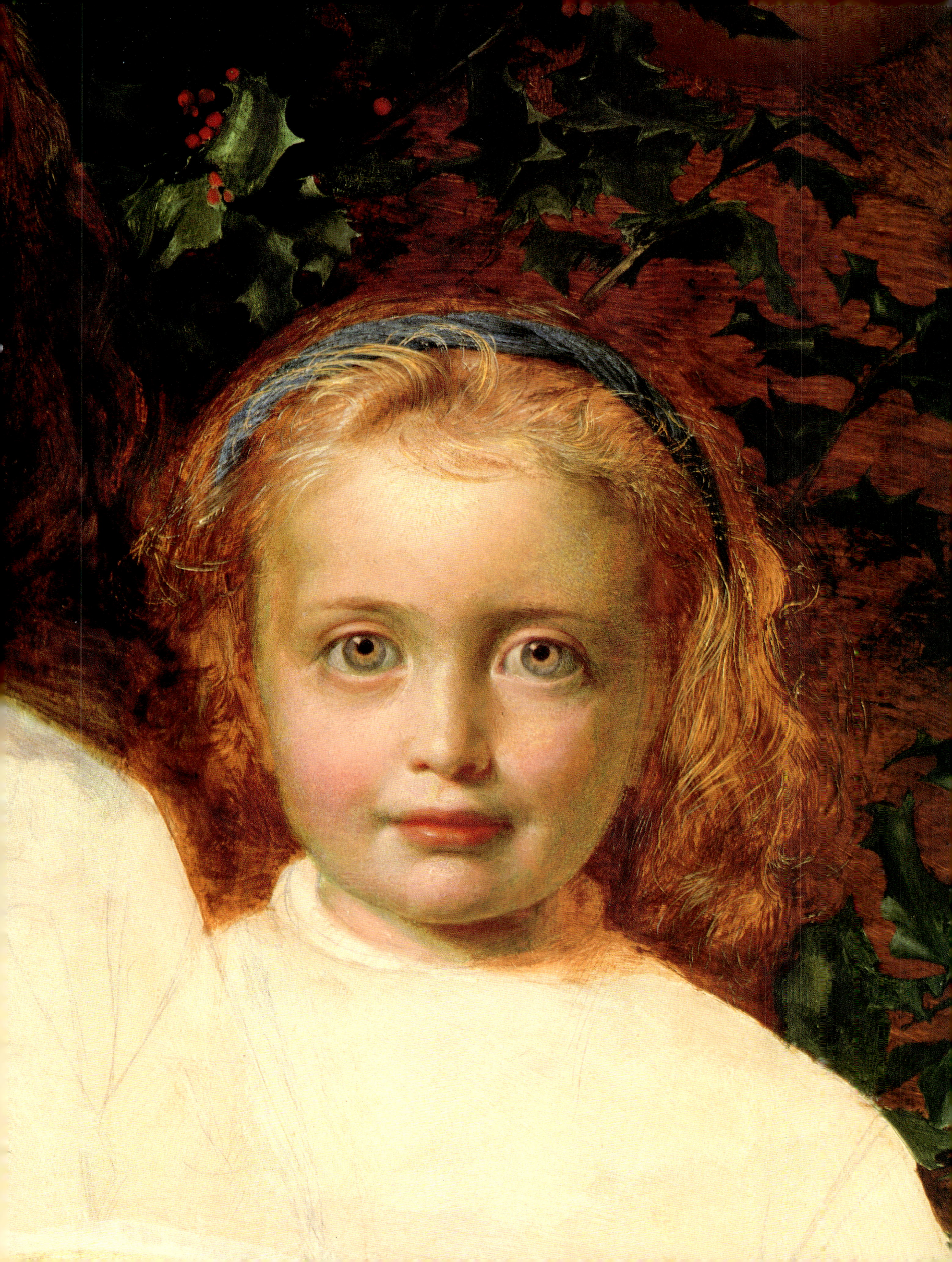

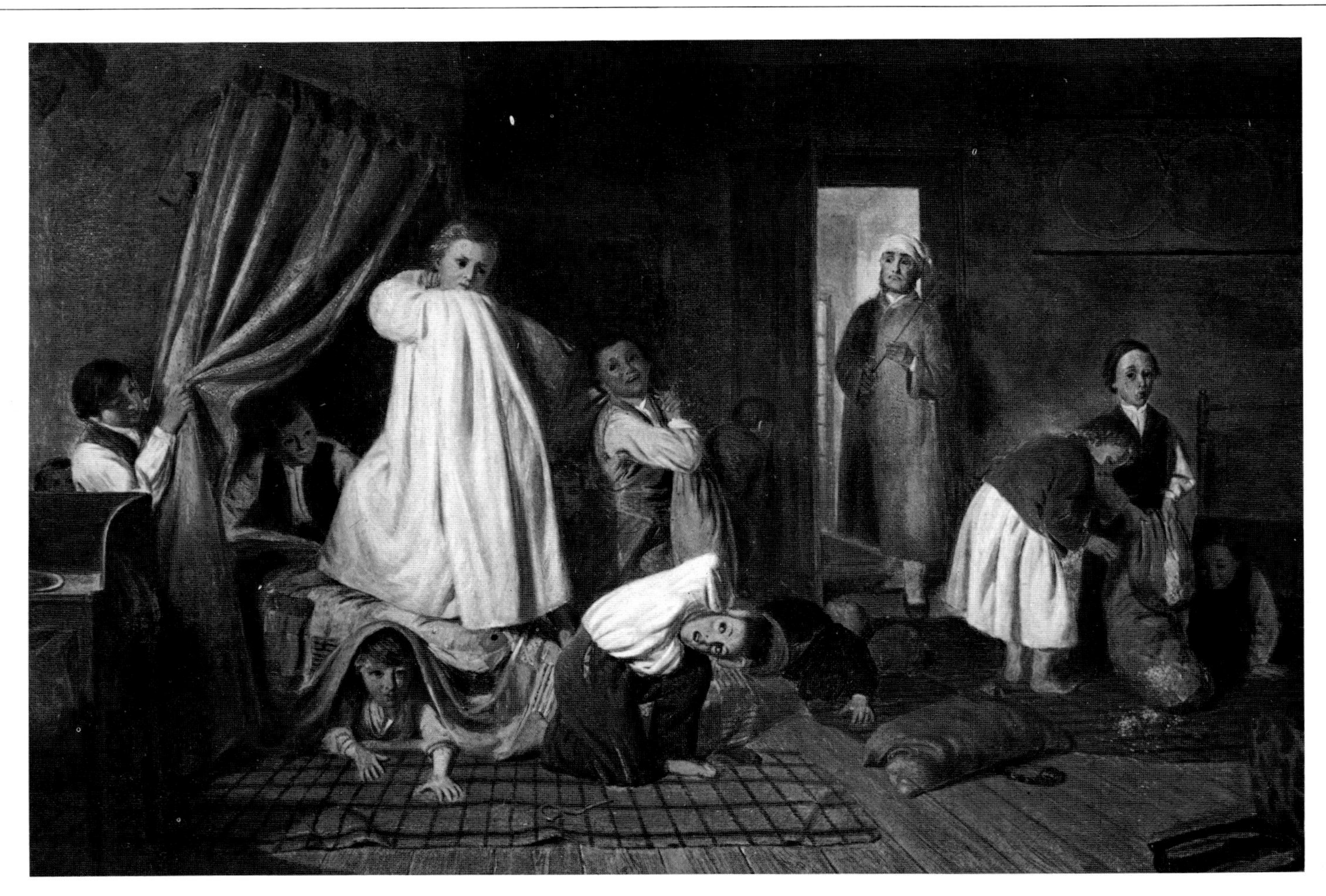

Plate 9

MATTHIAS ROBINSON (fl. 1856–1884)

*THE BATTLE OF THE BOLSTERS*, 1863

Oil on canvas, 11¾ × 17½″

Relatively little is known about this artist, who exhibited only three paintings at the Royal Academy in 1856, 1857, and 1863. However, he was a much more active contributor to the Society of British artists between 1857 and 1884, and many of the titles of his paintings—such as *The Careless Boy*, 1862, *Dear Dolly*, 1873, and *Keeping School*, 1881—suggest that these were images of children. Matthias Robinson seems to have doted on scenes of boys playing "siege" and "battle," and this work may be related or identical to one of the same title exhibited as a finished sketch at the Society of British Artists in 1871.

When it was exhibited at the Royal Academy in 1863, *The Battle of the Bolsters* was described by *The Art Journal* as a "good example [of] the school which follows after David Wilkie . . . derived from the Dutch . . . small in size, generally simple and often trivial in incident . . . and for the execution it may almost be said, the more detail the better." While an earlier critic had compared Robinson's work with the eminent Daniel Maclise, this one drew a parallel with the much better known Thomas Webster. Like Charles Hunt, Robinson may have had some contact with the Cranbrook Colony, but in the absence of definite evidence it still can be said that his genre scenes with children are inspired by the paintings of Webster, and Frederic Hardy in particular. Hardy produced many vignettes in which children were engaged in some activity when a grown-up suddenly arrives or approaches the doorway, and this is certainly the case here. The setting in *The Battle of the Bolsters* seems to be a boys' dormitory, the site of a different kind of mischief—taking advantage of a fellow student—in James Collinson's *Temptation*, 1855. There are several beds in the room, a washstand, and a map on the wall at right, and the young occupants are quite rowdy on the evening depicted. The group at right is probably putting back feathers that spilled from a pillow, while another child at left stands in his nightshirt atop his bed in order to barrage his rival with a blow from his pillow. Some of the boys are still dressed while others are in nightclothes; some actively participate in the game, others hide behind the curtain or under the bed. Perhaps the noise of voices or the fallen chair has aroused the teacher or headmaster, who arrives in robe and nightcap with a cane in hand. Apparently the boy hiding behind the door has failed in his function as lookout, and one can only imagine how much discipline the participants of the battle will receive in the way of a flogging or caning for their transgression.

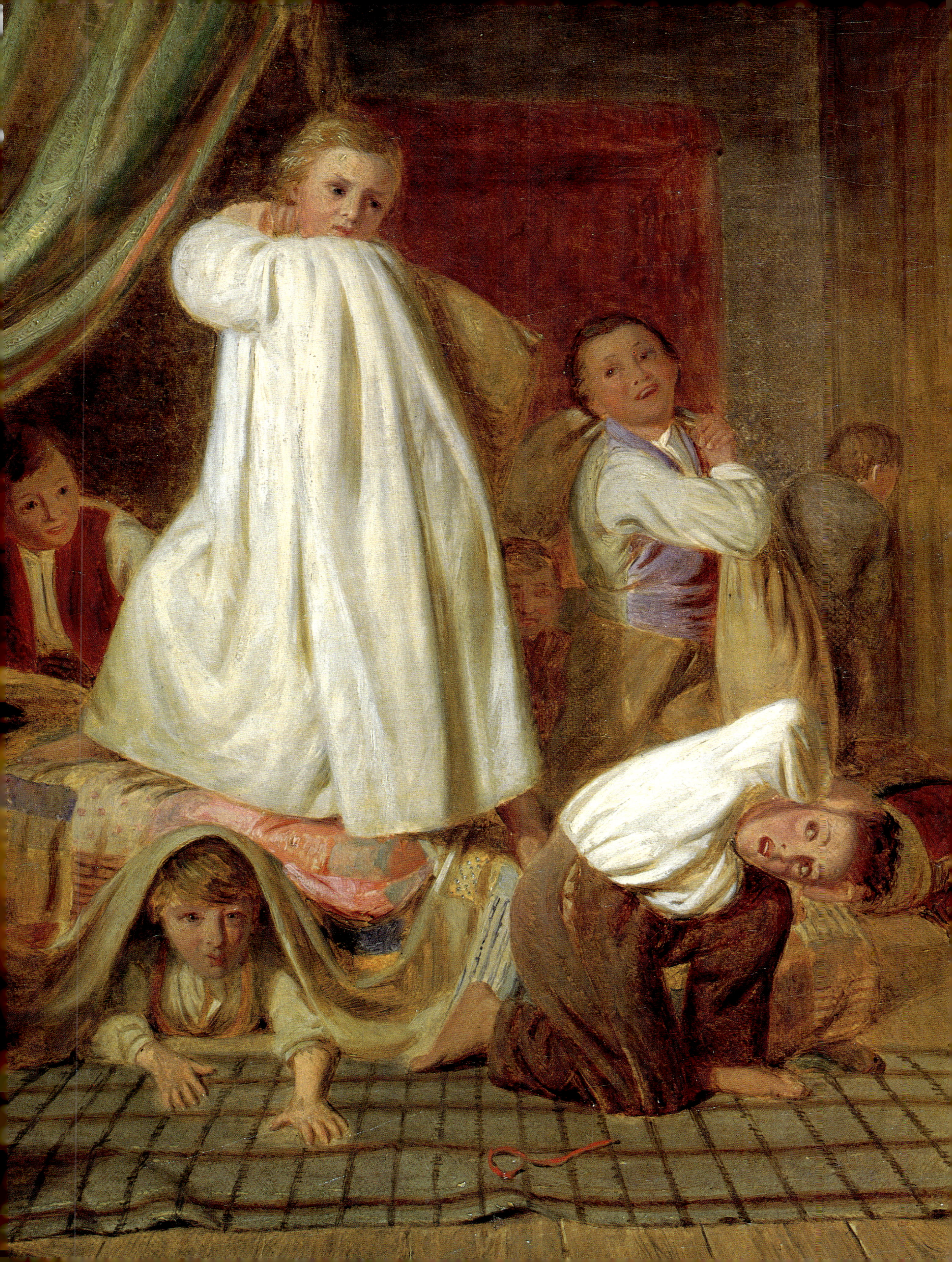

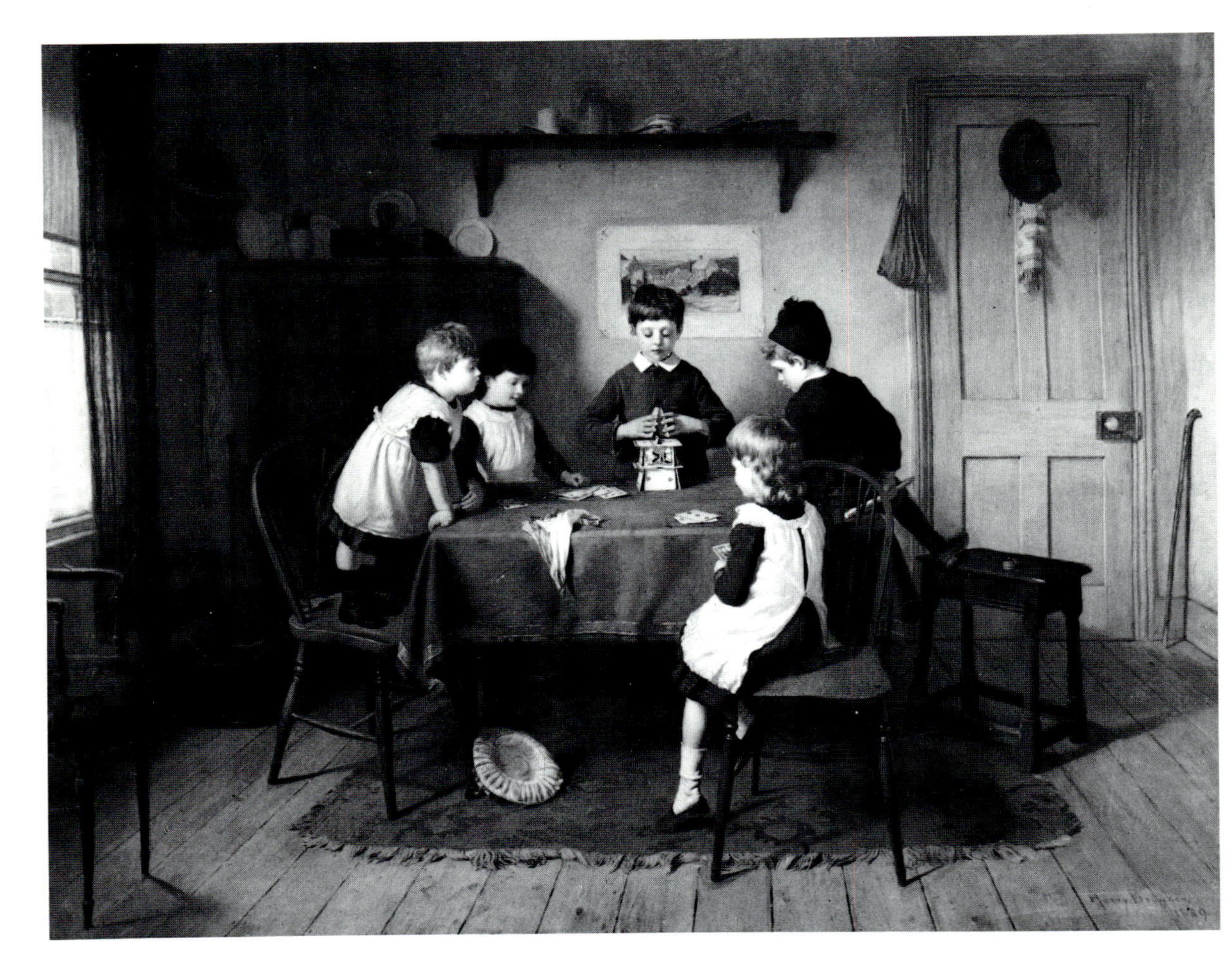

Plate 10

HARRY BROOKER (fl. 1876–1902)

*A CRITICAL MOMENT (A HOUSE OF CARDS)*, 1889

Oil on canvas, 28¼ × 36¼″

Little is known about this artist who flourished between about 1876 to 1902, exhibiting only one picture at the Royal Academy in 1876 and four at the Society of British Artists between 1878 and 1881. A recurrent theme in these paintings is that of children at play and, fittingly, Brooker lived for part of his career at an address called Child's Place on Earl's Court Road in London.

A painting such as *A Critical Moment* is reminiscent of Frederick Hardy's earlier representations of children, usually as they were involved in dramatic play at home, typically mimicking adult behavior and roles. The tabletop focus of the children's activities, as well as the types of players, and even the inclusion of construction pieces (in this case a few cards) were also used with a slightly different effect in Brooker's 1902 canvas, *Making a Kite.* Unlike Hardy's pictures, neither of these works by Brooker shows an adult suddenly materializing at the door to supervise the children's games or criticize their conduct; however, in *A Critical Moment* there is a walking cane near the door at far right that may allude to the missing adult authority. Boys and girls watch intently as one of them constructs a house of cards, most of the children standing or sitting in ways that middle-class adults would probably deem ungainly and improper. (Perhaps the hat fallen on the floor suggests the children's carelessness and lapse of decorum.)

It is not clear whether there are negative or ominous connotations intended here about the act of building a fragile house of cards, as there clearly are, for example, in the first part of Augustus Egg's *Past and Present* trilogy of 1858. In Dutch seventeenth-century art, children playing cards often generated negative associations of corruption, gambling, and deceit, especially in the realm of deception in the "game" of love. Here, however, the children attempt to create some balance and harmony in the midst of unruliness and disorder, and Brooker has emphasized the concentration of the youngsters by making the composition so symmetrical. Chardin and other artists have also depicted children in similar pursuits, which in this case may be construed as a purely childish pastime but also perhaps as an allusion to the transience of life, a little *vanitas* of the need for care and patience in creating a stable house of cards and a well-ordered existence.

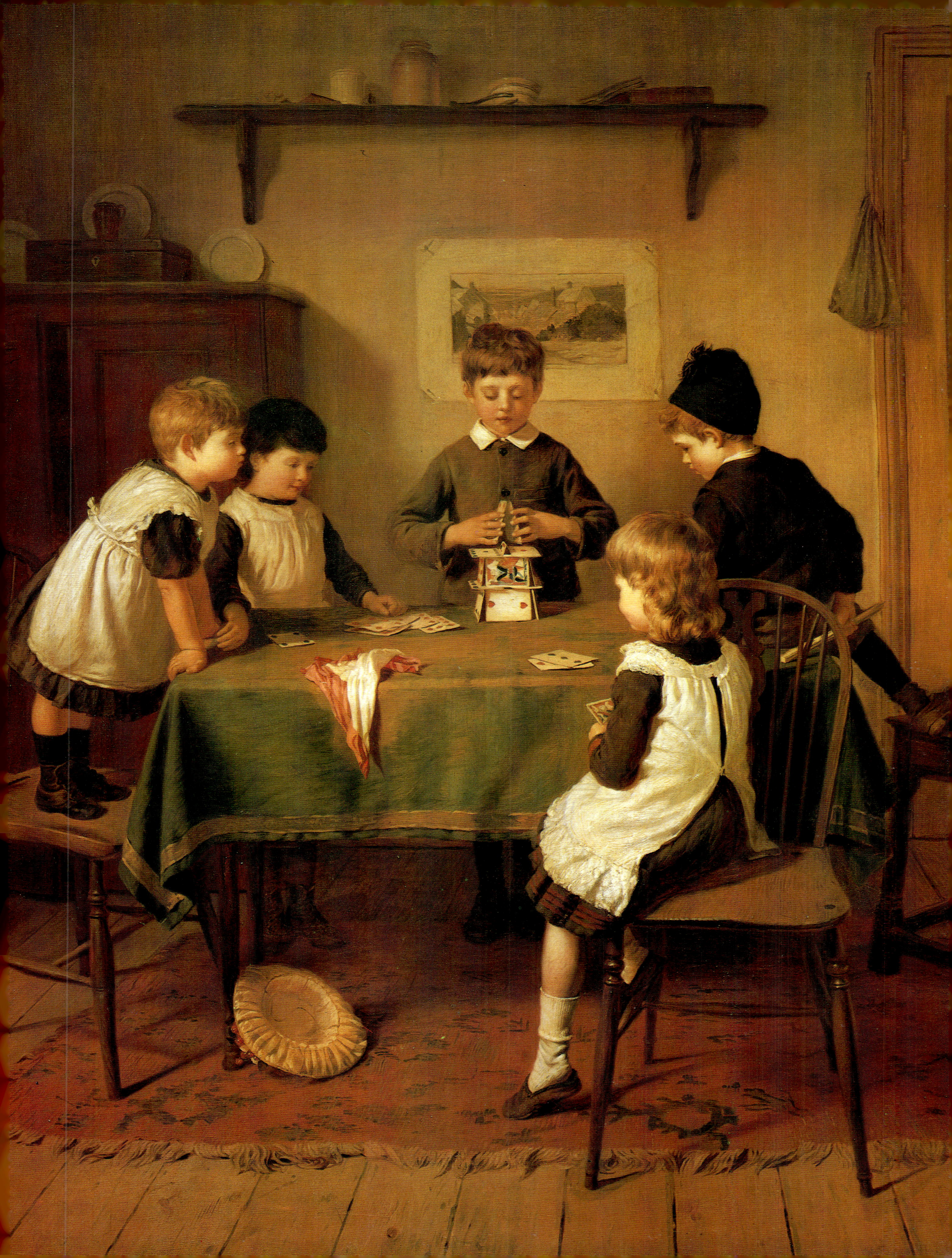

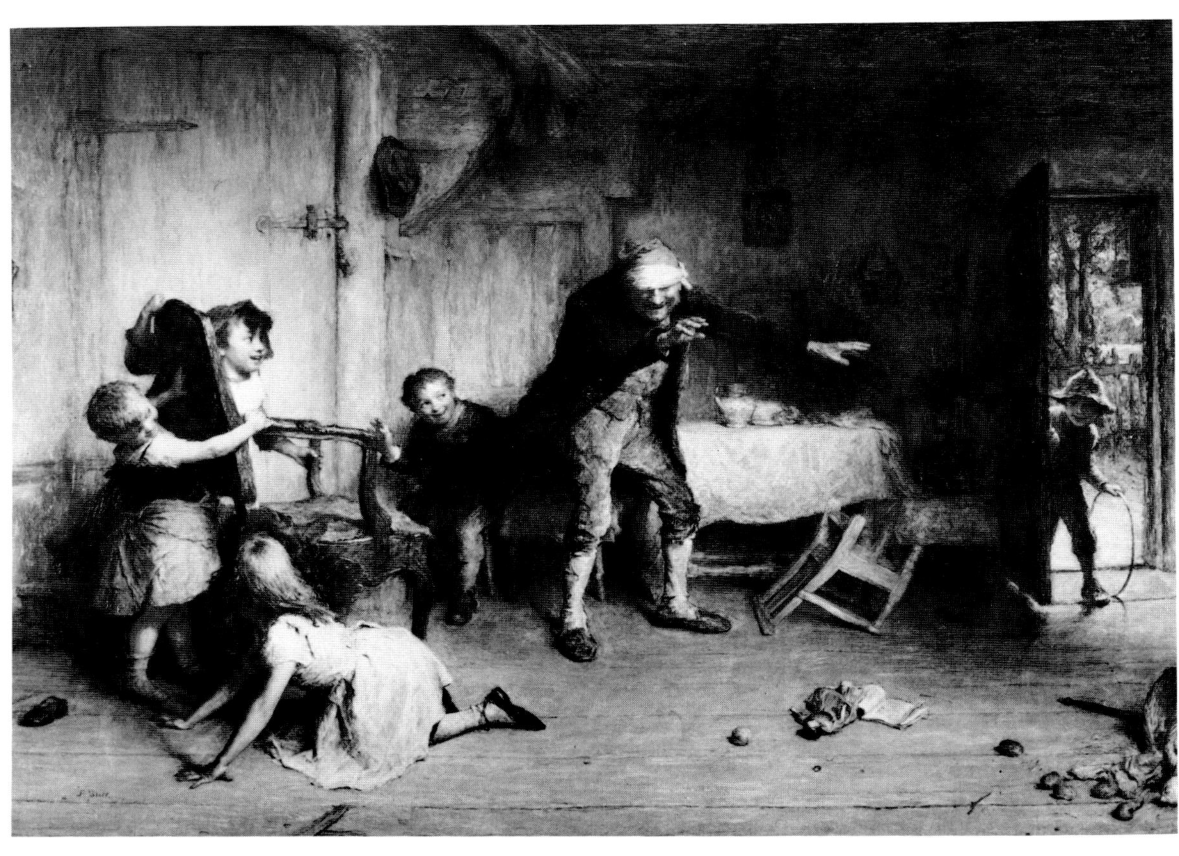

Plate 11

ALEXANDER H. BURR (1835–1899)

*BLIND MAN'S BUFF,* 1888

Oil on canvas, 30½ × 44¾″

Alexander Burr and his older brother both attended the Trustees Academy at about the same time, but Alexander worked with Robert Scott Lauder a few years longer than his sibling. Until about 1861 he remained in Scotland, where he painted numerous domestic scenes, thereafter moving to London and exhibiting regularly at the Royal Academy between the years 1860 to 1888. While the themes of some of his paintings were taken from literature or history—*The Escape of Queen Henrietta,* 1869, or *Sir Joshua Reynolds and Oliver Goldsmith,* 1882—Burr also created various narrative pictures of life on the streets of London, including the rather grim subject of *The Night Stall.*

In addition to other subjects, the artist also painted numerous anecdotal canvases with children as the primary actors and actresses, including *Shuttlecock* with a similarly spry old man involved in the action. He painted at least two versions of *Blind Man's Buff,* one of which was his final entry at the Royal Academy in 1888. Both are interior scenes of a cottage or rural classroom, in which a blindfolded old man plays an active game with several girls and boys. Indeed, the activity is so lively that chairs and myriad objects, including a peg doll, book, and a child's shoe, have all toppled and lie scattered on the floor. The children seem not at all in awe of their grandfatherly playmate as they laugh and scramble to hide behind doors and pieces of furniture.

The game was originally called Blind Man's Buff because the players buffeted and teased the "blind man" who had to tag and identify another player. This was a traditional English game played indoors or outside, and popular Victorian variations included the oddly-named Hot Cockles, Blowing Out the Candle, Buff with the Wand, Brother I'm Bobbed, Blind Postman, the Bellman, Cat and Mouse, Isaac and Rebecca, Alice, Where Art Thou?, and Squeak Piggy Squeak. Here the participants are children, but a more exciting game for adults was "Guessing Blind Man," for which the rules stipulated that a young gentleman had to find the lap of a young lady on which to sit.

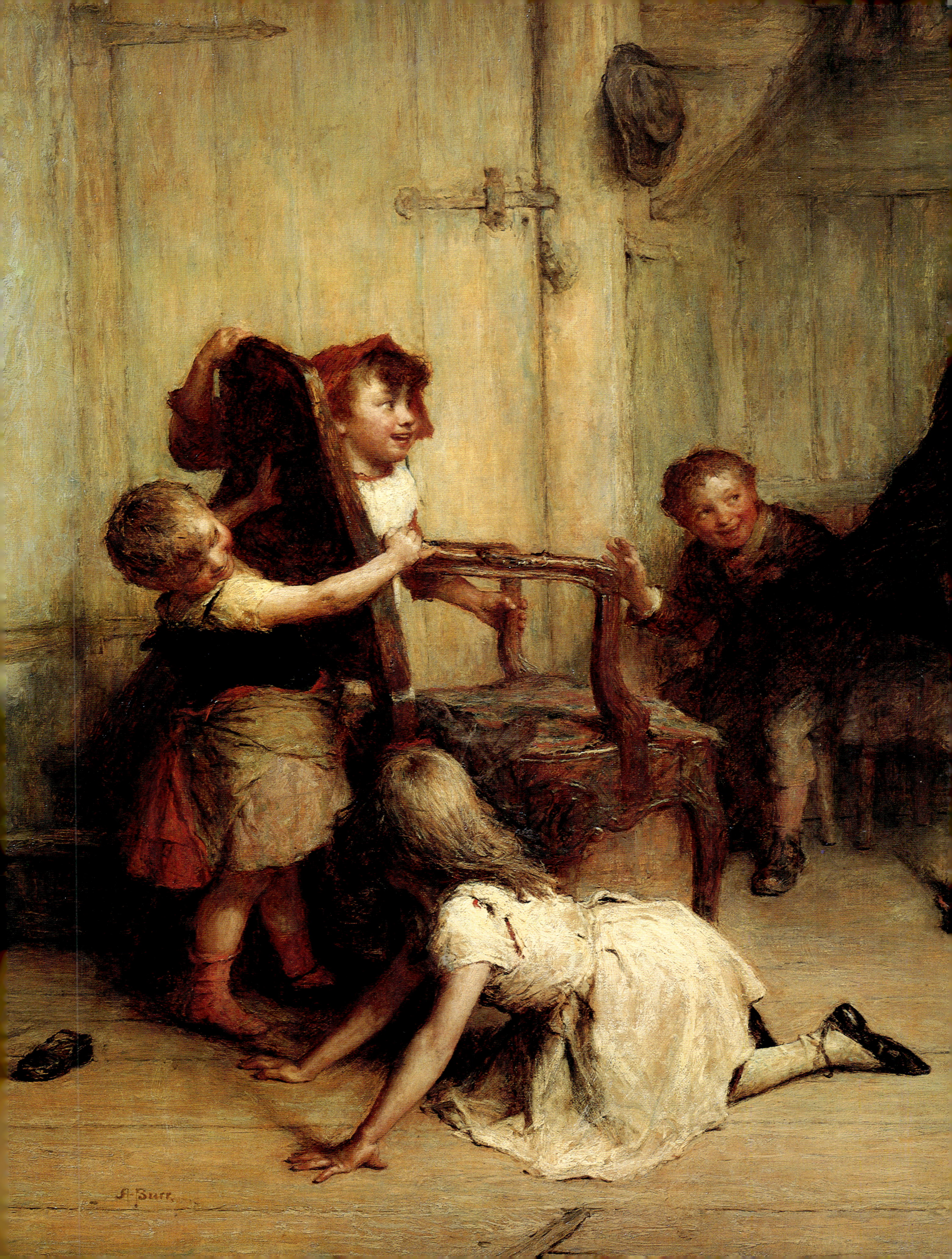
A. Burr.

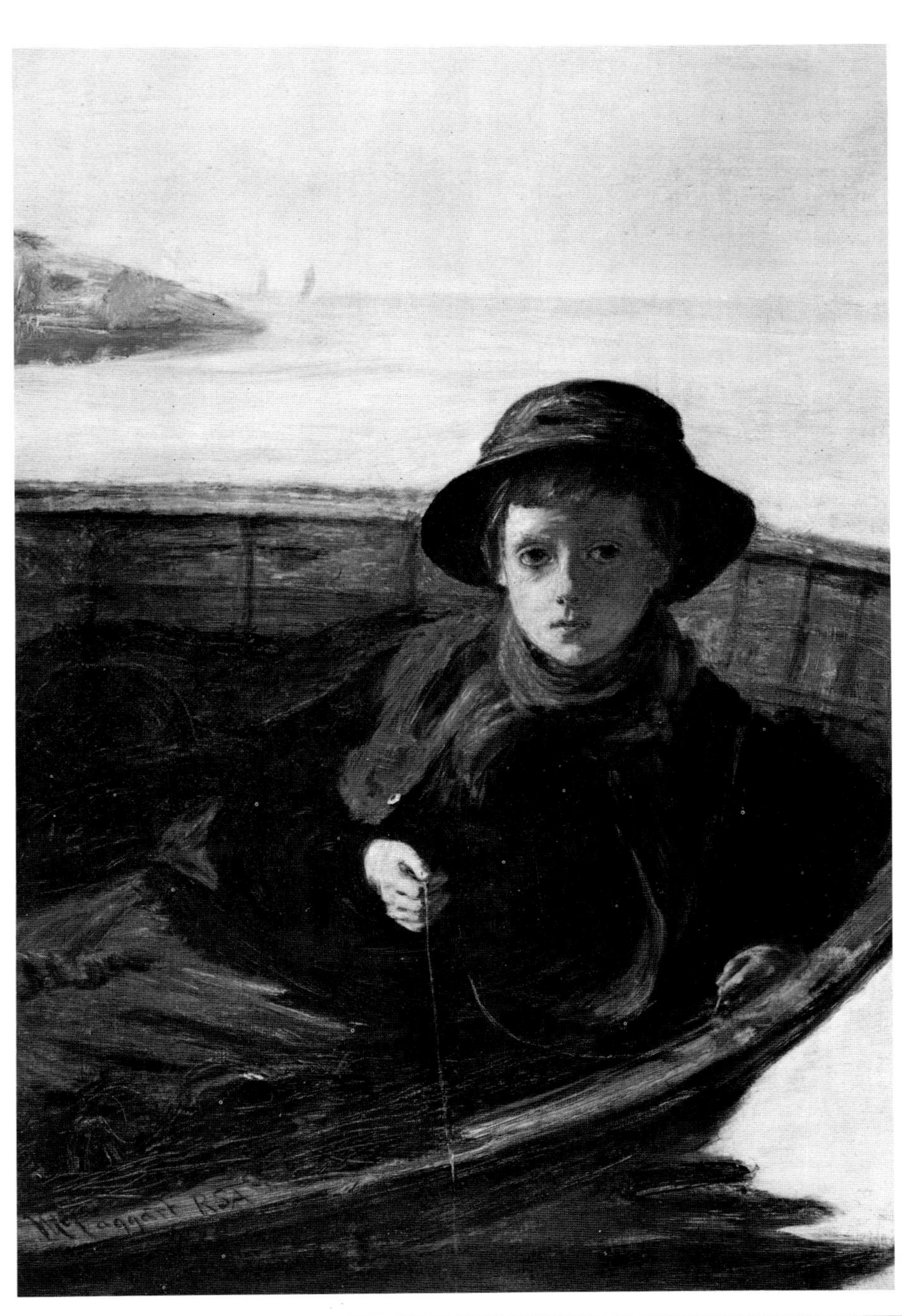

Plate 12

WILLIAM McTAGGART (1835–1910)

*THE FISHERBOY*, 1870

Oil on canvas, 16½ × 12″

Born in Scotland in a place not far from the sea, William McTaggart left home in order to study with Robert Scott Lauder at the Trustees Academy in Edinburgh from 1852 until 1859. In Edinburgh he came into contact with several fellow artists destined for eminence, a group that included William Quiller Orchardson and John Pettie. McTaggart began exhibiting at the Royal Scottish Academy in 1855, was elected a full member in 1870, and showed there regularly until 1895. At the same time he was active in the Royal Scottish Watercolour-Society and also exhibited at the Royal Academy in London between 1866 and 1875.

While his early works were typically genre or literary pictures (with subjects taken from Tennyson's "Enoch Arden," for example), often manifesting the influence of the Pre-Raphaelites, at about 1870 McTaggart turned increasingly to the sea and to the lives of the fishermen as a source of inspiration. It was about that time that he began to spend summers at Tarbert on Loch Fyne, and by 1889 he had built a glass-roofed studio in an isolated village not far from the sea so he could devote himself more fully to his study of the effects of light and water. Although he apparently did not see the work of the French Impressionists until the 1890s, his own later works evoked comparison with theirs, mostly because of the expressive and free brushwork that became more and more characteristic of his style.

In *The Fisherboy* McTaggart reveals his earlier penchant for depicting the everyday life of fisherfolk along the coasts of Scotland as well as prefiguring his later looser, fresher way of applying paint and of translating light into sparkling visual effects. The artist, himself the parent of ten offspring, often portrayed children sympathetically, and here he depicts a young lad intent on fishing from a boat (McTaggart himself loved boats and sailing). Sometimes his children frolic together in sunny landscapes, yet here the boy seems to be alone and content in his small craft. As in the title of another work of 1870, *Adrift*, he seems to be floating between the shore and the distant sea, suspended between childhood and adolescence.

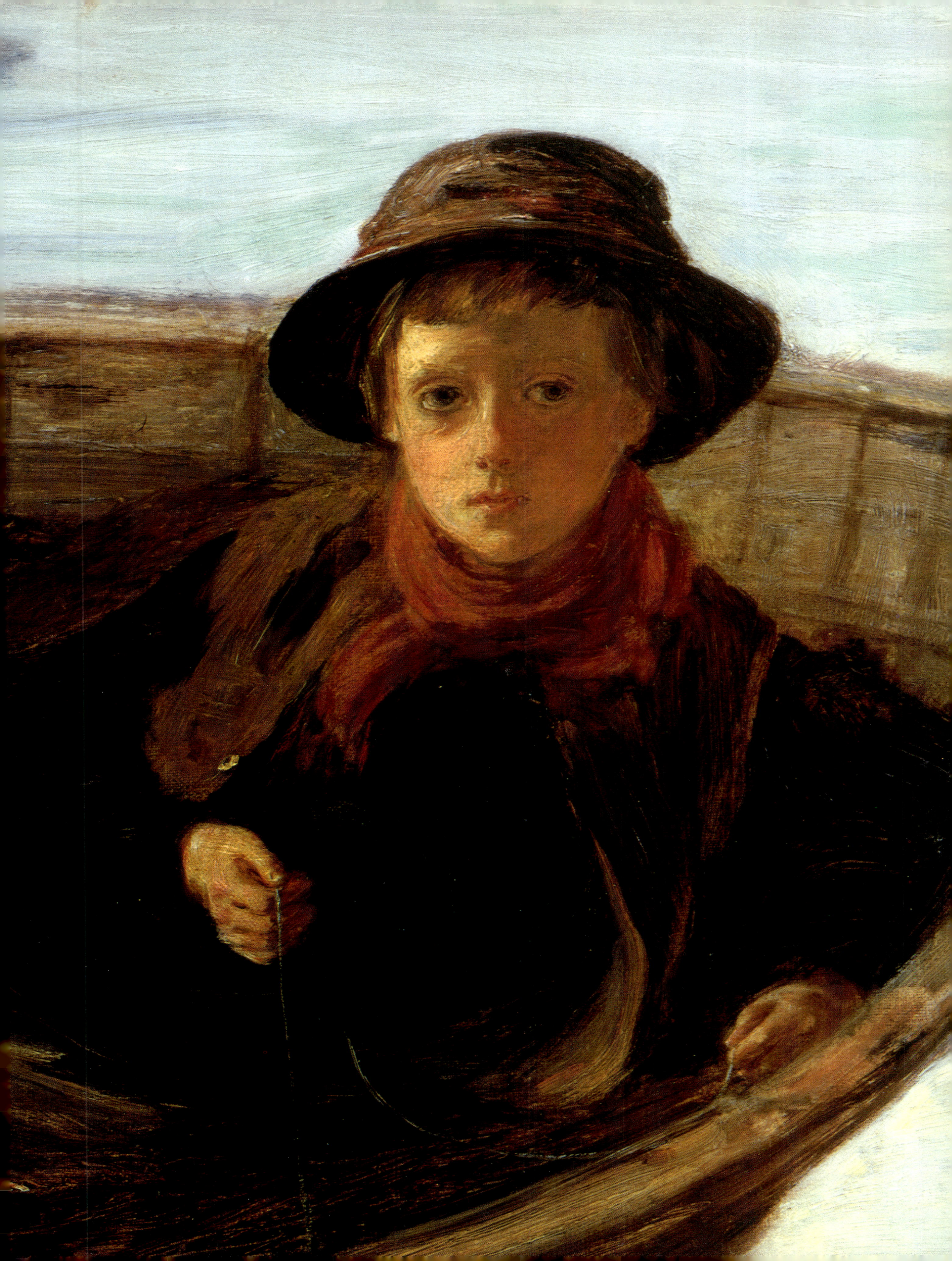

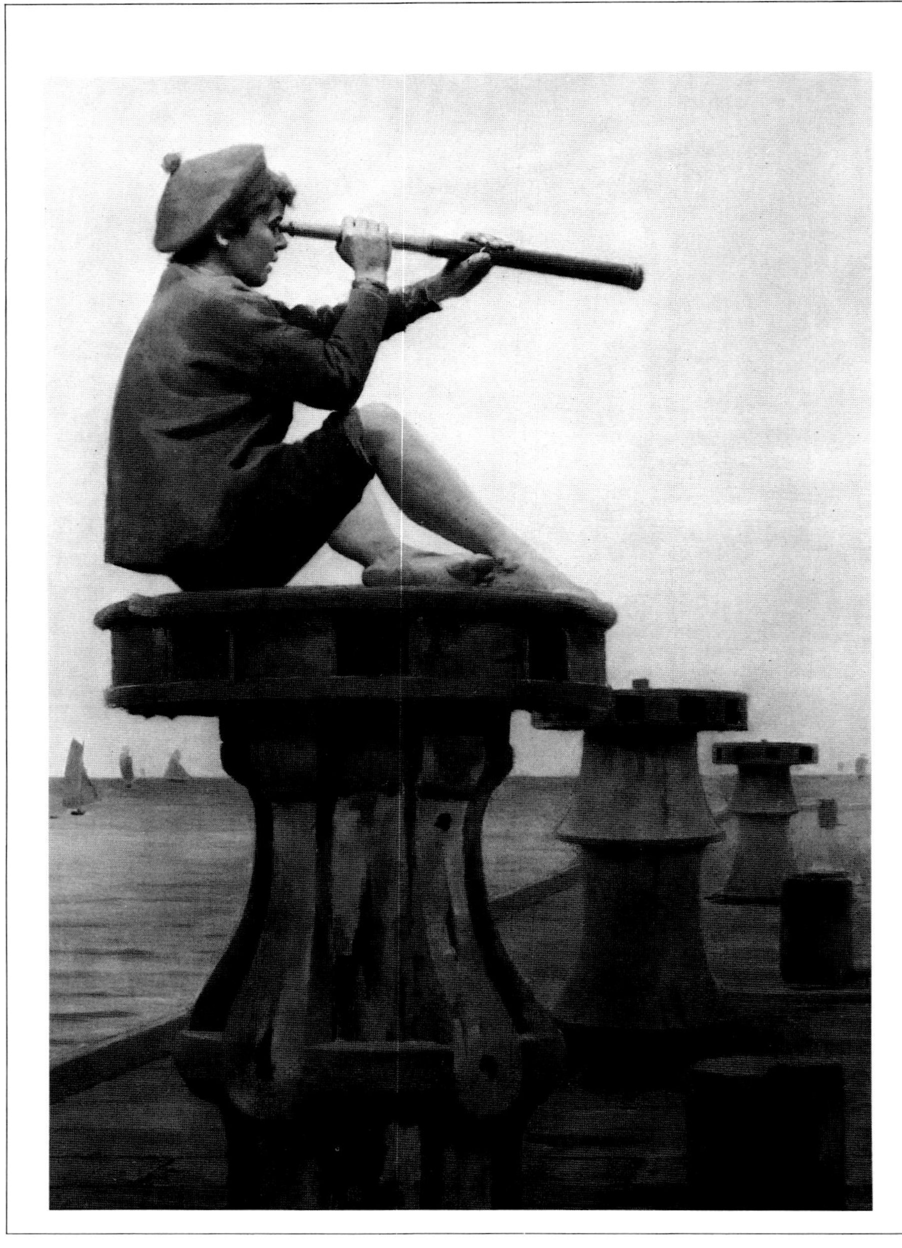

Plate 13

STANHOPE FORBES (1857–1947)

*SHIP AHOY*, ca. 1900–10?

Oil on canvas, 30 × 21″

Born in Dublin, Stanhope Forbes later studied at the Royal Academy Schools and in Paris under Léon Bonnat. In 1881 he painted in Brittany with Herbert LaThangue in order to work *en plein air*, a commitment to outdoor painting that he upheld throughout his career. After working in a French fishing village Forbes looked for a counterpart in England, and this he found in the fishing village of Newlyn; from about 1884 onwards he became the central figure of the Newlyn School, counting among his colleagues William Langley, Thomas Gotch, Fred Hall, and Henry Tuke. Although he did not like the Royal Academy "system," Forbes exhibited there regularly and was elected an Associate in 1892, a full Academician in 1910; among his greatest critical successes there were *A Fish Sale on a Cornish Beach*, 1885, and *Forging the Anchor*, 1892. In 1899 he and his wife, fellow artist Elizabeth Armstrong Forbes, opened a school of painting in Newlyn and spawned a second generation of the Newlyn School.

*Ship Ahoy* probably dates from the artist's later career after 1900. He convinced many Newlyners to pose in the streets or by the water, and perhaps such was the case here with the barefoot boy and his telescope. Forbes had earlier been inspired by the style and subject matter of the French artist Bastien-Lepage, and even in this late work the Frenchman's lightened palette and preference for everyday figures from contemporary life seem likely influences.

Forbes's continuing interest in light and atmosphere are also conveyed in *Ship Ahoy*, where he has combined careful observation with the modern Newlyn brand of realism, especially the immediacy of effect and the freshness of color. In terms of subject, the work is akin to that of other Newlyn artists, such as H. E. Detmold's *Departure of the Fishing Fleet*, 1889, and of Forbes's own *Off to the Fishing Ground*, 1886. Here there is only one rather undramatic figure, who looks out to sea in a moment of calm—not impending danger—perhaps dreaming of an exciting life as a sailor or fisherman. In the early Edwardian years Forbes also exhibited at the Royal Academy works with such nautical titles as *Against Regatta Day*, 1906, and *A Fleet in Sight*, 1911; it is possible that the latter painting is the same as or related to *Ship Ahoy*.

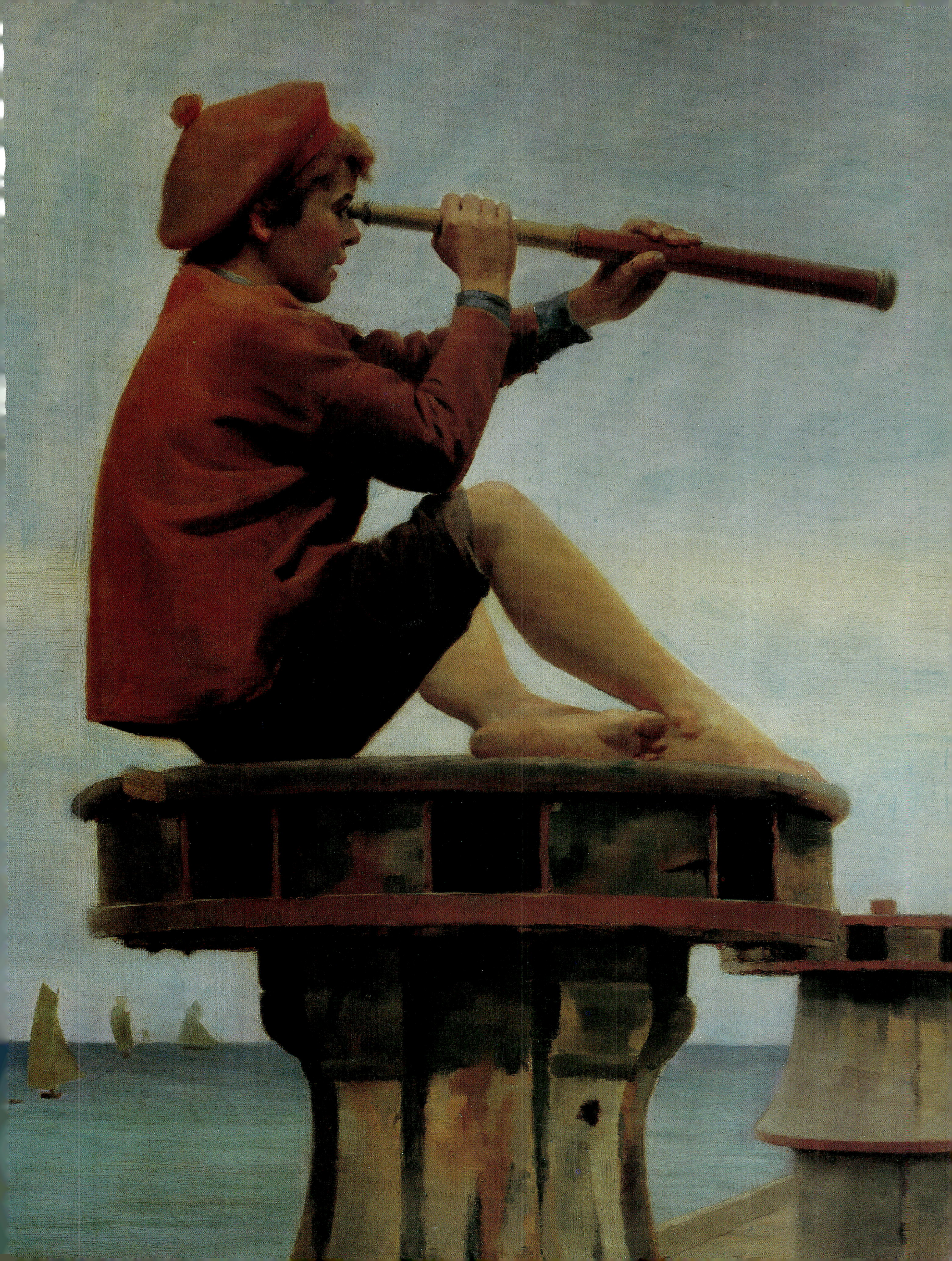

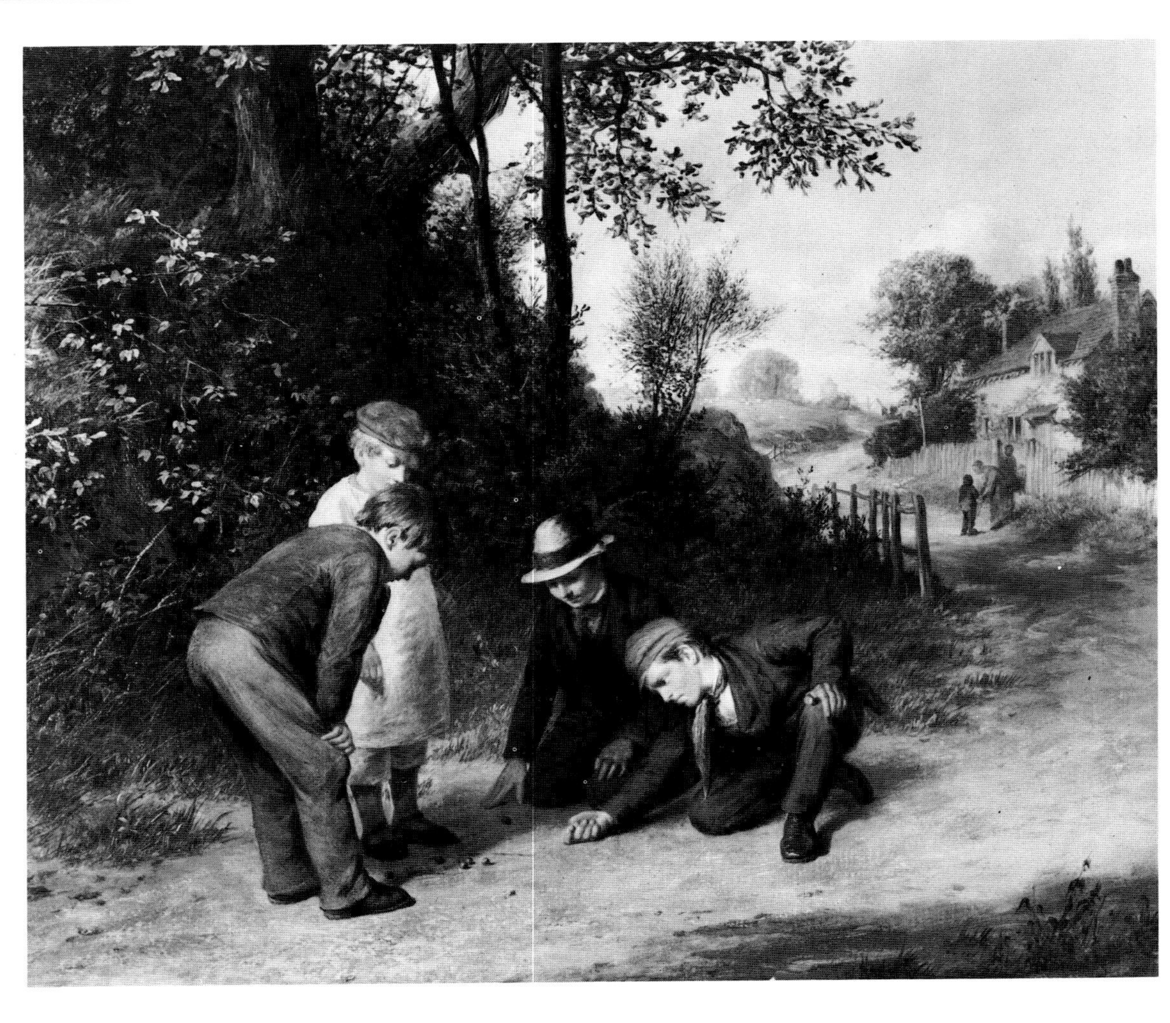

Plate 14

WILLIAM BROMLEY (fl. 1835–1888)

*PLAYING AT MARBLES*, ca. 1871

Oil on canvas, 17 ×23″

William Bromley was named after his grandfather, an artist who distinguished himself as an engraver as well as a painter. The grandson exhibited nearly two hundred paintings at the Society of British Artists, the Royal Academy, and the British Institution, and his long career spanned the years 1835 to 1888. Almost all of his entries can be classified as historical pieces, literary scenes, or genre pictures, and in the latter category numerous titles suggest that the protagonists were children. Among these are several schoolroom vignettes, including *Late at School*, 1855, and others such as *Queen of the May*, 1853, *Playing at Buttons*, 1863, and *The Young Boat Builder*, 1864 that evoke various pastimes of the young.

*Playing at Marbles* may have been the canvas exhibited at the Society of British Artists in 1871; the title describes the age-old game that was very popular with boys. Marble-playing was so widespread, in fact, that foreign competitors began to manufacture and market marbles at a cheaper price for lower-class children, prompting *Everybody's Magazine* to lament in 1876 that these inexpensive foreign products (ironically often made with child labor) were woefully inferior in quality. Many boys collected various sizes, patterns, and hues of marbles, saving their best agates or "aggies" (or their "swirlies" or "clearies") for especially important games; poorer children played with plain clay marbles. This subject was also treated by other Victorian artists such as Charles Hunt in *Playing at Marbles*, 1848, as well as in John Haynes's 1863 canvas entitled *Taking Aim*.

The subject of *Playing at Marbles* may owe a debt to seventeenth-century Dutch painting, perhaps in this case to Quirin Brekelenkam's *A Game of Marbles* with its similarly crouching figure at the right caught at the moment of taking aim with his favorite marble on the smooth ground. It is not clear whether the Dutch—or the Victorians—attached some didactic meaning to this game of skill, some message about winning, hoarding, or the like, but the depiction of young boys (or adult men, who in some villages played marbles in competition) in an outdoor setting, engaged in this intense activity with players, onlookers, and adversaries all present, appeared frequently in both seventeenth- and nineteenth-century canvases.

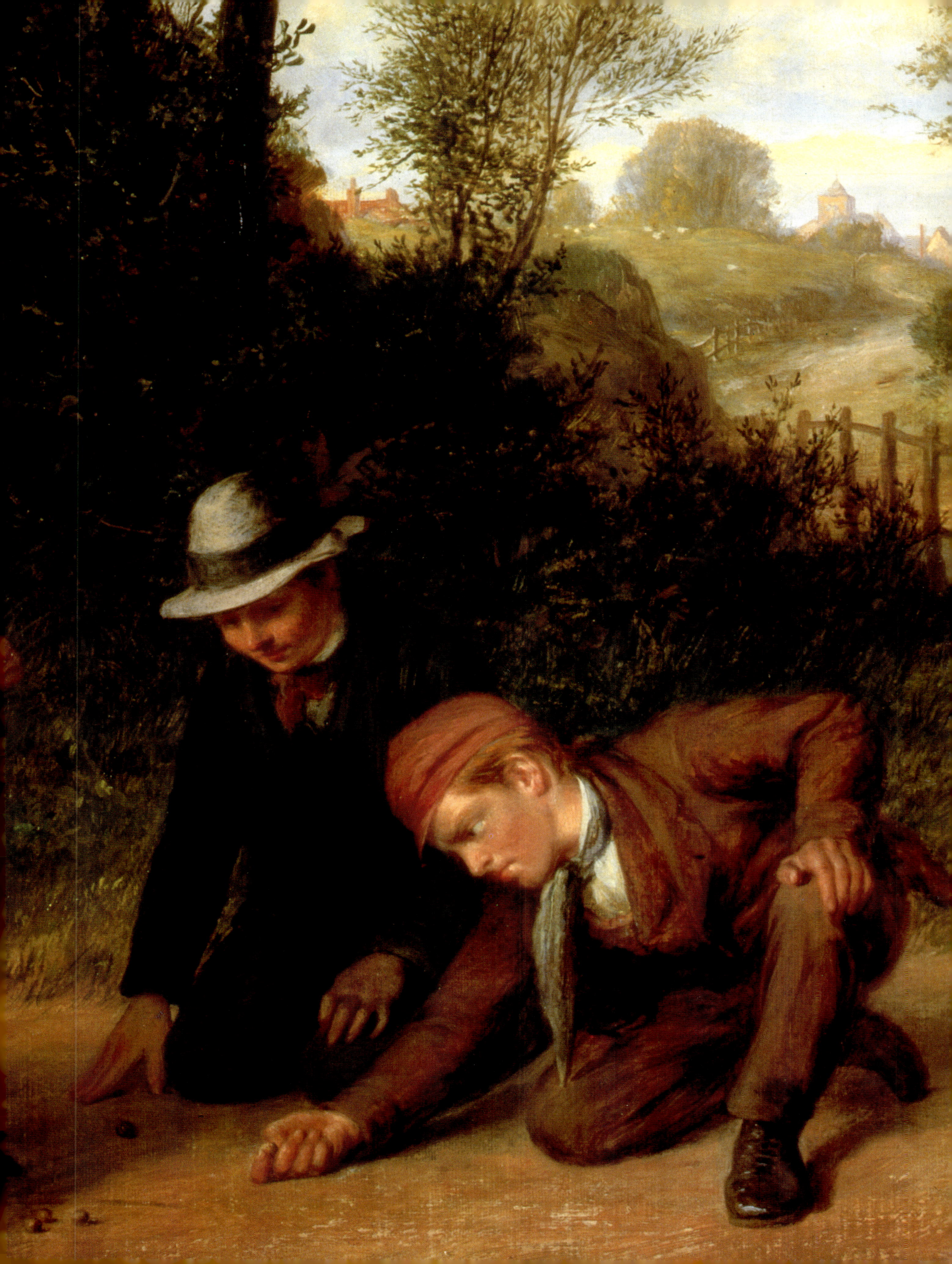

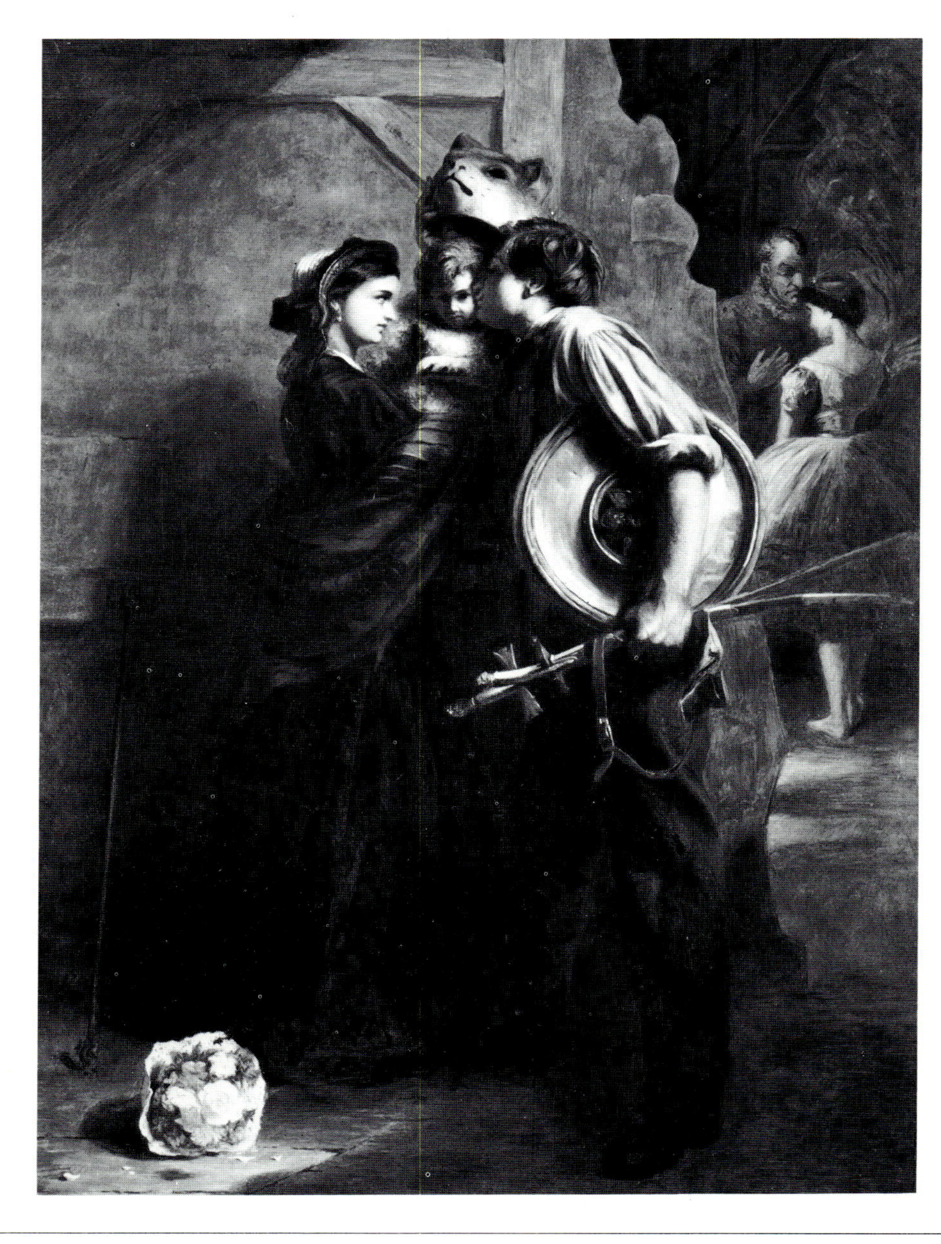

Plate 15

LASLETT J. POTT (1837–1898)

*PUSS IN BOOTS—BEHIND THE SCENES*, 1863

Oil on canvas, 24½ × 18½″

A child prodigy of sorts, Laslett Pott studied at Carey's Art School in London and became a pupil of the Scottish genre painter Alexander Johnstone. Pott's first Royal Academy picture, *Effie Deans*, 1860, drew its inspiration from a novel by Sir Walter Scott, and many of his subsequent paintings were based on literary sources or historical events. Among works in the latter category were *Mary Queen of Scots being led to Execution*, 1871, *Charles I leaving Westminster Hall after his Trial*, 1872, *The Trial of Queen Catherine*, 1880, and *Napoleon's Farewell to Josephine*, 1891.

Pott's first success at the Academy, where he exhibited until 1897, was *Puss in Boots*, and he was fortunate in having this picture hang "on the line," a premium location, especially for a novice. The subject derives from the fairy tale by Charles Perrault that was popular among Victorian readers, who enjoyed the exploits of the clever cat who helped his poor master achieve a fortune. Here the artist takes us backstage where a child, still in the costume of Puss, is being greeted by his parents after a performance. While acting troupes and young performers were often classed as amusing but vulgar, one critic for *The Reader* in 1863 thought the scene was a realistic one and that "there is something sad and always touching in sacrificing the innocency [sic] of children on the altar of theatrical necessity. Mother and child . . . are alike too good for their business; and the kiss of the father may arise from the prompting of his heart to tear off the catskin and boots from the child, if the necessity for the ugly disguise could be avoided."

Another writer in 1877 speculated that the scene was a Christmas pantomime, the behind-the-scenes viewpoint allowing spectators to see "the clown gossiping with Columbine between the slips, and a man putting the mask of a gigantic pussycat on the head of a little child." The parents are both tenderly solicitous of their little one, but how much a Victorian viewer would have thought about the difficult life of the actor—rather than merely sympathizing with the child's predicament—can only be surmised. Perhaps as a result of the success of *Puss in Boots*, a few years later Pott sent *Fire at a Theatre* to the Royal Academy exhibition of 1869. While the former was humorous in mood, *Fire at a Theatre* depicted a frantic life-or-death rescue of a child from a raging conflagration.

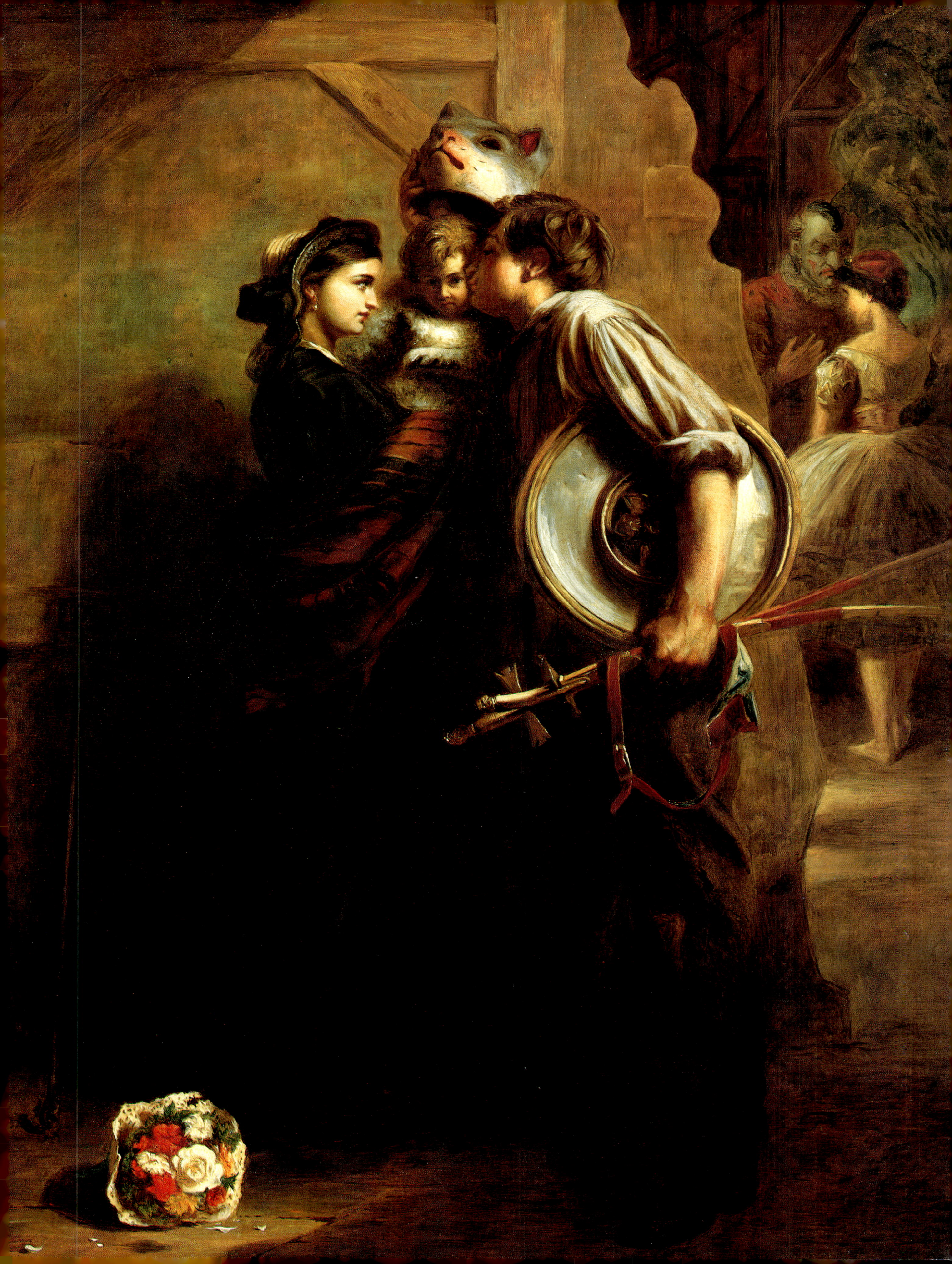

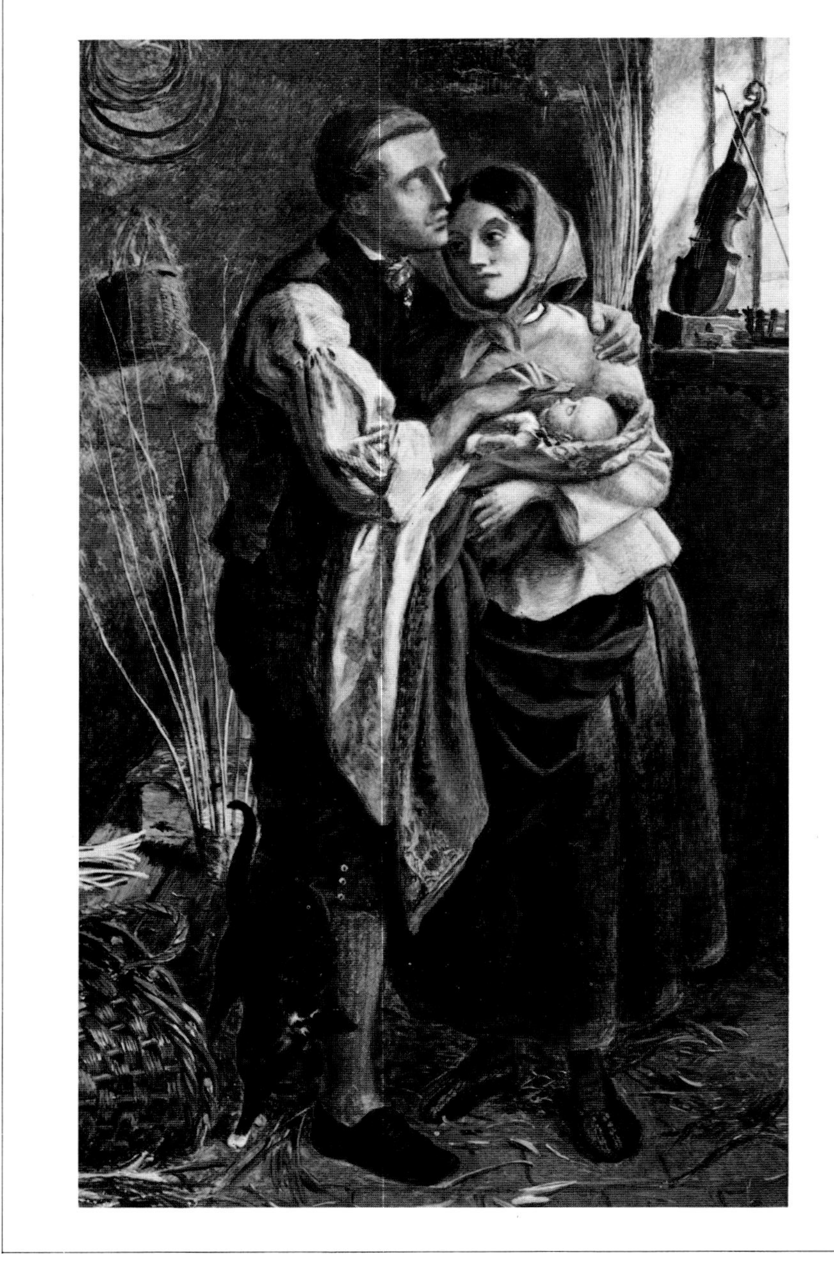

Plate 16

MICHAEL FREDERICK HALLIDAY (1822–1869)

*THE BLIND BASKET-MAKER WITH HIS FIRST CHILD*, 1858

Oil on panel, 10 × 6″

The son of a captain in the Royal Navy, Michael Halliday also held a post in the House of Lords before he started his career as a painter in the 1850s. He may have been influenced in this decision by his friend John Everett Millais, for the two men went on vacations and hunting trips together in the English and Scottish countryside in 1854, 1855, and again in 1861. Halliday shared a London studio briefly with another Pre-Raphaelite brother, Holman Hunt, and seems to have known all the other members of the Brotherhood as well. He occasionally accompanied Hunt to Royal Academy exhibitions and was a diligent correspondent when Hunt went to the Holy Land, even traveling almost to Constantinople to bring his sick friend home in 1855. Halliday's *The Measure for the Wedding Ring*, 1856, won him some praise at the Royal Academy and was thereafter engraved.

In *The Blind Basket-Maker With His First Child*, which was an Academy entry in 1858, the subject is a married peasant couple in their humble home. All around are reminders of the blind man's lost sense—the light streaming in the window and especially the arrival of a child he can only touch but never see. Accordingly, his wife tenderly places his hand near the child's face so he can feel its contours, and with his other hand he gently touches her shoulder as well. All around are the tools of a basket-maker's trade and his manual creations; viewers might have speculated that the father is wondering whether his first offspring will also be blind. While one of the man's five senses is impaired, the others have been enhanced by the sound of the songbird in the cage above, the music produced by the violin at the window, and the furry warmth of the family cat rubbing against the man's leg.

Given Halliday's friendship with both Hunt and Millais, it is not surprising that this painting shows the influence of both artists. The pose seems reminiscent (in reverse) of the lovers in Millais's famous *Huguenot* painting of 1852, and there is also a debt to the poignant mood of that picture. There is also an echo of Hunt's *Claudio and Isabella* of 1850, especially in the detail of the sunlit–barred window with a musical instrument placed nearby.

In terms of critical response at the 1868 Royal Academy exhibition, *The Literary Gazette* pronounced this work "the most successful that this fast-rising artist has yet exhibited, and deservedly praised for its truth and vigour united." On the other hand, *The Athenaeum* did not like the man's face, and especially criticized his wife's foreign-looking slippers, "which are certainly not English."

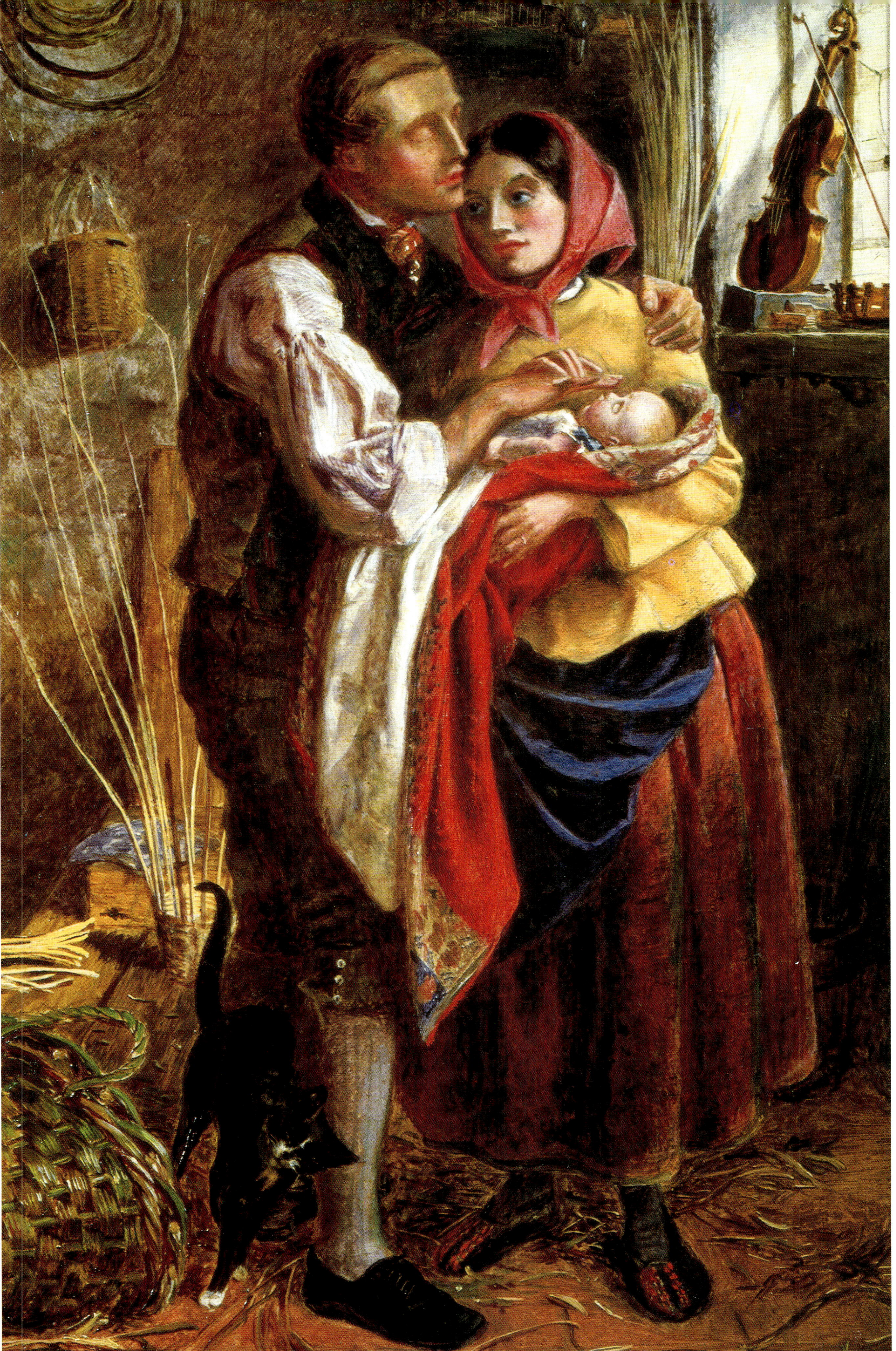

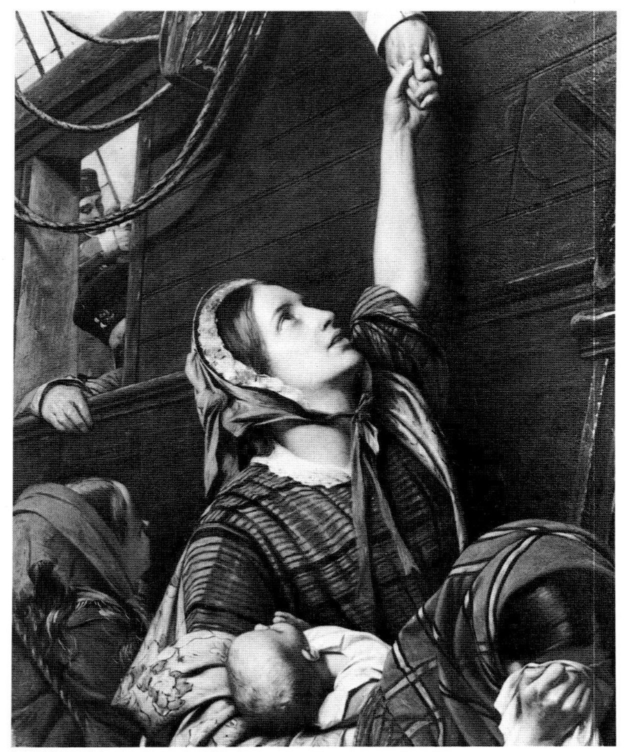
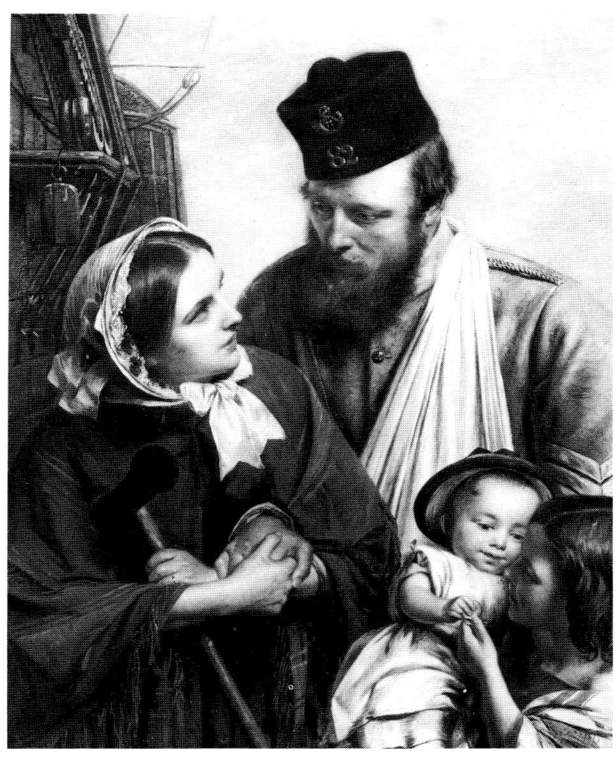

Plate 17

HENRY NELSON O'NEIL (1817–1880)

*EASTWARD HO!—HOME AGAIN*, 1859

Oil on canvas, 20½ × 34″

Born in Russia to English parents, Henry O'Neil studied at the Royal Academy schools in 1836 where he met Augustus Egg, William Powell Frith, and others who would ultimately form the membership of an avant-garde, anti-establishment group called "the Clique." Many of O'Neil's paintings were inspired by historical, religious, or literary sources and had titles such as *Paul and Francesca of Rimini*, 1842, *Ruth and Boaz*, 1844, *Mozart's Last Moments*, 1849, *Rosalind and Celia*, 1856, and *Michael Angelo*, 1870. His first resounding success at the Royal Academy, to which he contributed from 1838 to 1879, was *Eastward Ho!*, August, 1857, a canvas that dealt with the military decision to send British troops to suppress the Indian Mutiny and rebellious sepoys in various Indian cities. Other artists (and many journalists) treated this theme, but O'Neil's painting seems to have caught the particular fancy of the public and was extravagantly praised in the pages of *The Athenaeum*, *The Art Journal*, and *The Times*, among others.

O'Neil followed this painting in 1859 with a sequel entitled *Home Again*, and the tremendous popularity of the pair (which were also engraved by William Turner Davey) created a demand for numerous replicas by the artist. O'Neil later tried to recapture their success with *The Parting Cheer*, 1861, and *Before Waterloo*, 1868, but these never eclipsed his popular Royal Academy entries of 1858 and 1859.

The FORBES Magazine Collection owns smaller versions of both of the famous original canvases, but in this *Eastwrad Ho!—Home Again*, the composition is significantly altered. Instead of a horde of friends and family welcoming the returning soldiers, the focus is on one family. (This modification was perhaps a reaction to criticism that the original had been too crowded.) William Mulready, Noel Paton, and other painters of the time also chronicled the homecoming of the veteran. O'Neil's wounded hero is tenderly greeted by his wife, who holds his crutch and takes his hand while sharing a loving gaze with her husband. At this moment, neither parent looks at the children, a little girl taking care of a toddler who was only an infant in the departure scene. Although the man is an injured hero, yet even more than his bravery, it is the sanctity of the family that is celebrated in this painting. Family harmony, paternal achievement, and pride are qualities often communicated in Victorian paintings, and such ideas undoubtedly met with approval from bourgeois viewers. Moreover, the children in this ordinary "holy family" represent not only the veteran's kin, they also symbolize the future of England in a new generation that must deal with subsequent issues and consequences of war and peace.

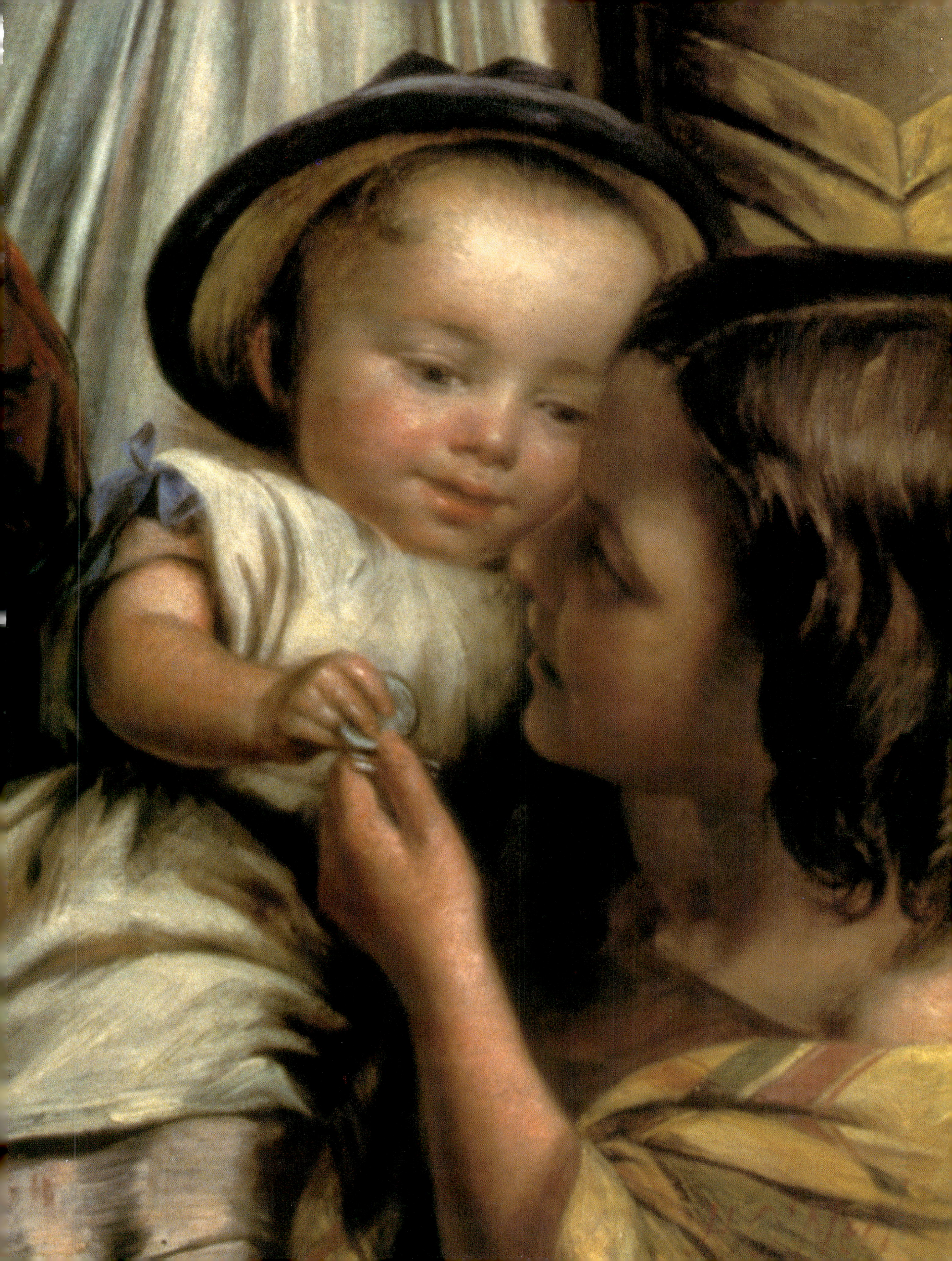

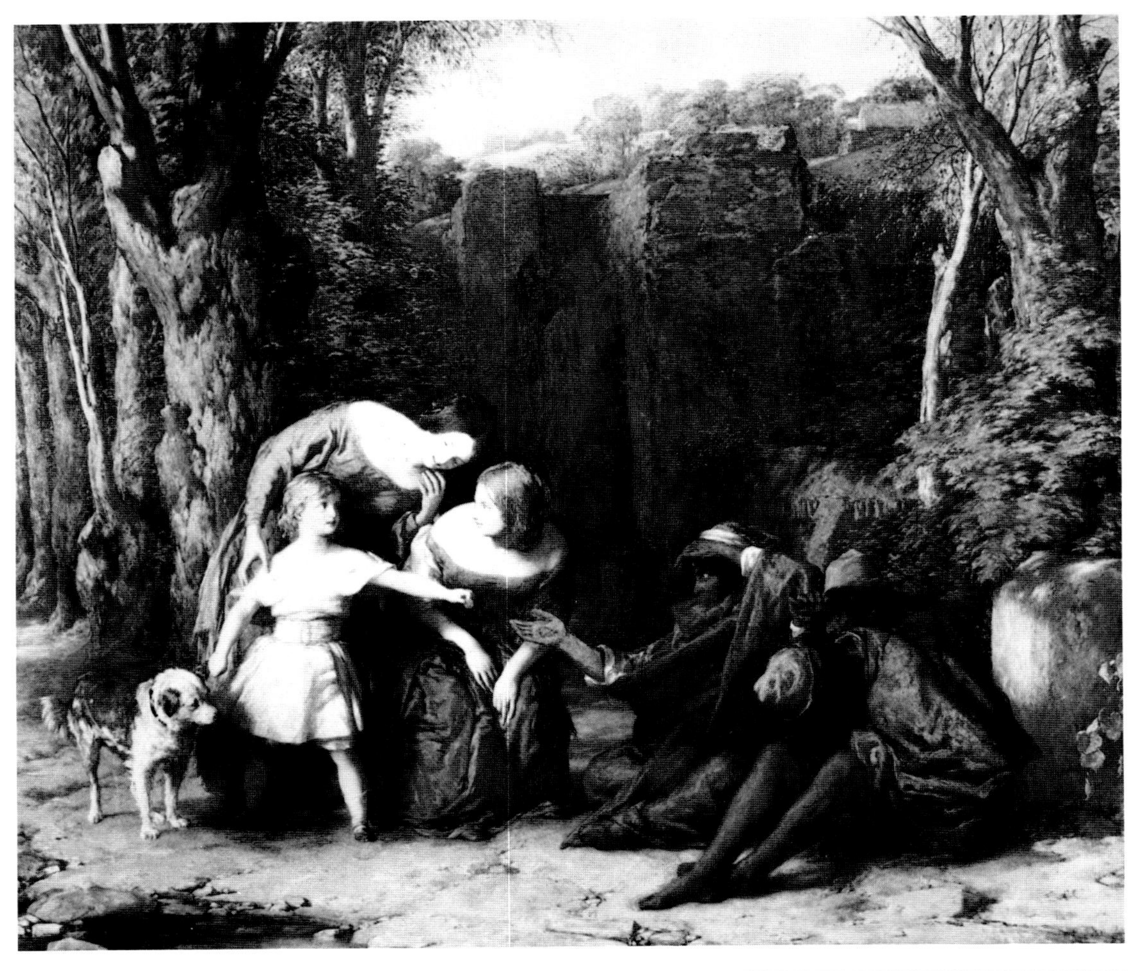

Plate 18

WILLIAM MULREADY (1786–1863)

*TRAIN UP A CHILD IN THE WAY HE SHOULD GO, AND HE WILL NOT DEPART FROM IT*

Proverbs 22:6, 1841

Oil on panel, 25¼ × 30½″

A prodigy who entered the Royal Academy schools at the age of fourteen, William Mulready initially produced some genre scenes reminiscent of David Wilkie's (and also some handsome landscapes) before acquiring his own stylistic approach to domestic subject matter. His first critical success was *The Fight Interrupted*, 1816, and this portrayal of a vicar halting a boys' quarrel set the standard for many subsequent depictions of children, including *A Boy Firing a Cannon*, 1827, *The Last In*, 1835, and *First Love*, 1840.

*Train up a Child* (for which there are related drawings at the Victoria and Albert Museum) illustrates a scriptural precept (Proverbs 22:6) and is presumably intended as a sermon in paint about the importance of teaching children a moral lesson—to help the less fortunate of the world. Representations of rustic charity had been treated by earlier artists such as Thomas Gainsborough and Francis Wheatley, and here the same convention of women and children helping the needy is reiterated. However, in this painting the effect is somewhat different because the objects of charitable attention are not Victorian Britons but foreign Lascars or Indian soldiers, who inhabit what is literally the darker side of the canvas, much as their benefactors come from a path of light. A woman encourages the child to offer his alms to the beggars, but the hesitant boy seems afraid of the mendicants crouching nearby. Yet, as one critic noted in the *Fine Arts Quarterly Review* in 1863, the Lascars also seem fearful; "notice . . . their slow, oriental motion of uncovering, and of imploring salutation and reverence, the arms silently outstretched to receive the half-affrighted boy's gift. Their strange eyes, motions, attitudes, and costumes are expressed so powerfully as to . . . almost make us share it, thus giving dignity, force, and tragic interest to the picture." While this painting, like Mulready's *The Lesson*, 1859, is in part a statement about adult responsibility for the religious instruction of a child, to modern viewers there may also be a covert message conveyed about British imperialism and its paternalistic attitude towards Indians and other persons of color.

According to his close friend and former pupil John Linnell, Mulready was a good father to his numerous children, and Mulready's biographer, Frederic Stephens, suggested as well that the artist's own life "illustrated the force of the injunction to parents that they should train their children in the way they should go." Stephens also reported that Mulready considered *Train Up a Child* his masterpiece, and he himself repaired the painting for its first owner Thomas Baring (a well-known banker and philanthropist who paid a high price for it) after the work was damaged in a fire in 1853.

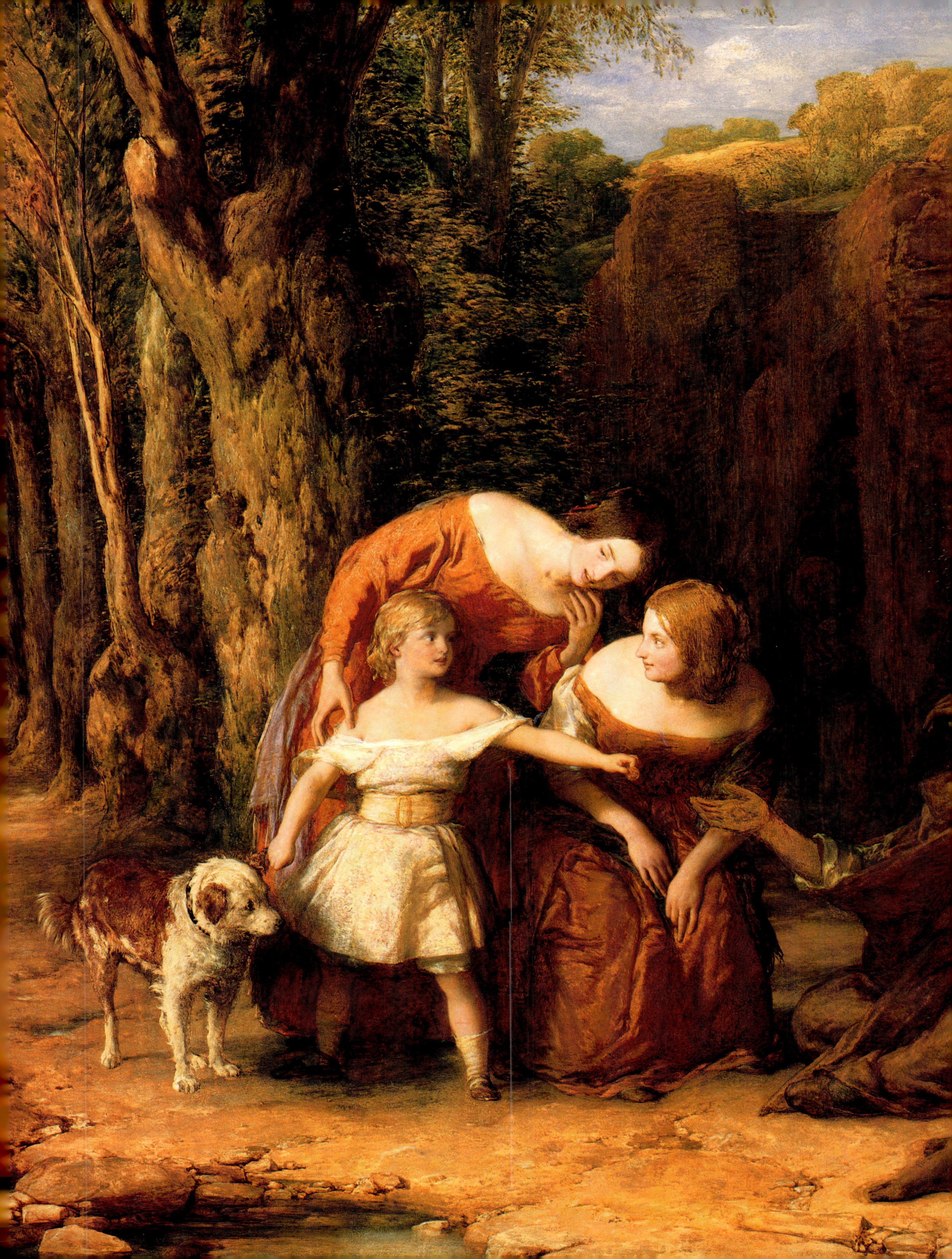

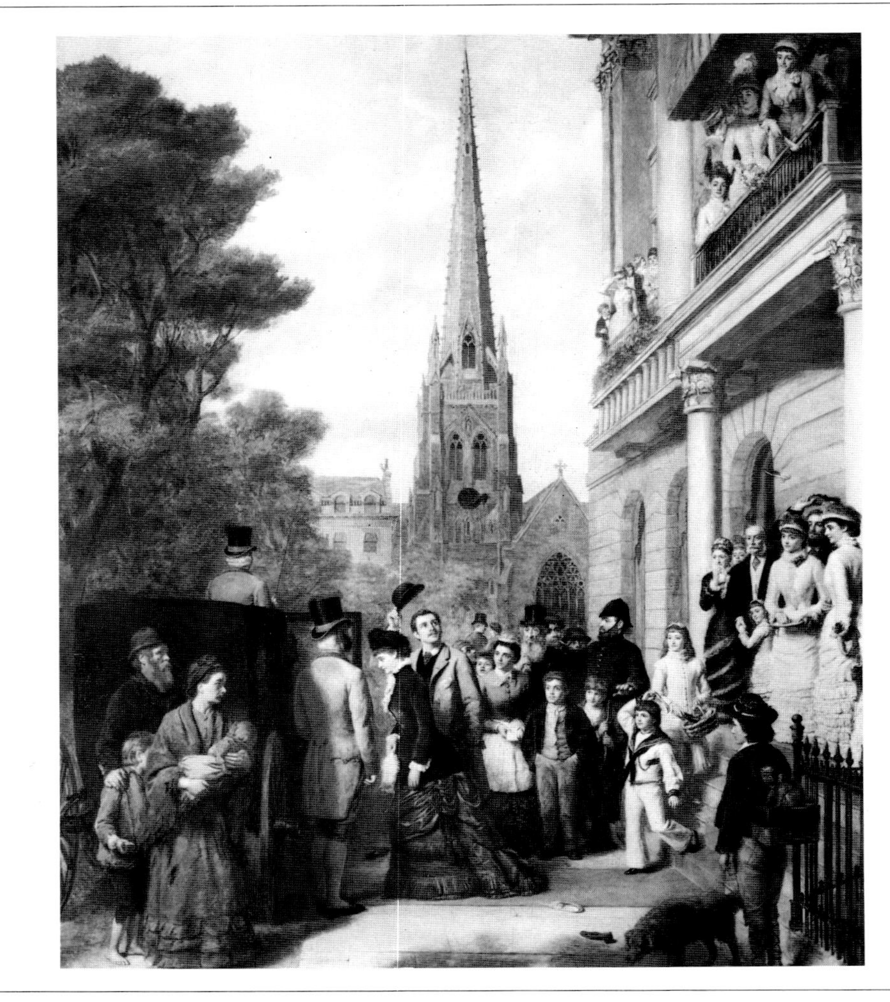

Plate 19

WILLIAM POWELL FRITH (1819–1909)

*FOR BETTER, FOR WORSE,* 1881

Oil on canvas, 61 × 49″

A member of the Royal Academies of London, Stockholm, Vienna, and Belgium, William Powell Frith became an artist largely because of parental pressure, although he was later to become very rich in this career. He contributed dozens of Academy entries between 1840 and 1902, but it was *Life at the Seaside,* 1854, and *Derby Day,* 1858, that had a galvanizing effect on the public. These lively panoramas of contemporary life were followed in 1862 by *The Railway Station,* an extremely popular painting that fetched a very high price when the engraving rights were sold. One of his paintings was included in the Centennial Exposition in Philadelphia in 1876, and prints after Frith's most famous canvases—those already mentioned in addition to the didactic series entitled *The Road to Ruin* and *The Road to Wealth*—became well known in England and America.

*For Better, For Worse* was exhibited at the Royal Academy in 1881; it was lampooned in *Punch* cartoons and compared by critics in *The Illustrated London News* and *The Athenaeum* with the verisimilitude and success of Frith's previous scenes of everyday life. The artist commented in his autobiography that the subject of departing newlyweds was based on a scene that he had actually witnessed in Cleveland Square in London. On the steps and the balcony above, the upper classes quite literally preside, while on the pavement a throng of street urchins, a group of beggars, a Jewish old clothesman, and a youthful organ grinder with his monkey gather to watch the couple enter the waiting brougham. The title, a phrase from the Church of England marriage service, seems to underscore various levels of irony. These are the words the bride and groom promise to heed in their life together, and yet it has been suggested that the bridegroom may be doffing his hat at his former lady love among the assembled bridesmaids on the balcony, a situation paralleled by Frith's own maintenance of two households—one with a wife and the other with a mistress, with offspring from both women. Moreover, the words also reflect the plight of a destitute couple and their family at left, whose marriage has sadly ended "for worse" in the streets of London. The two worlds of haves and have-nots almost collide, yet there is a gap of distance and apparent lack of sympathy between those who are affluent and those who are destitute; this range of social classes was a recurrent theme in Frith's paintings. The presence of a church and its spire in the background makes the sanctity of the new union (and the possible old liaison with a mistress) as well as the injustices of life for those who are impoverished all the more ironic. Victorian courtship and nuptial rituals are also preserved in this painting, especially in the tossing of shoes at the newlyweds, an old custom that originally symbolized the transfer of "right" and authority from the bride's father to her husband by the exchange of one of her slippers.

As for the children in this painting, Frith recorded that he had difficulty with several of the models. The boy near the constable fainted at one point, his hands never leaving his pockets, while the little Italian organ grinder apparently had difficulty dealing with the monkey. The artist finally became so exasperated that he (the father of nineteen children) later commented, "Little children are maddening; but commend me to the most terrible of those in preference to a monkey."

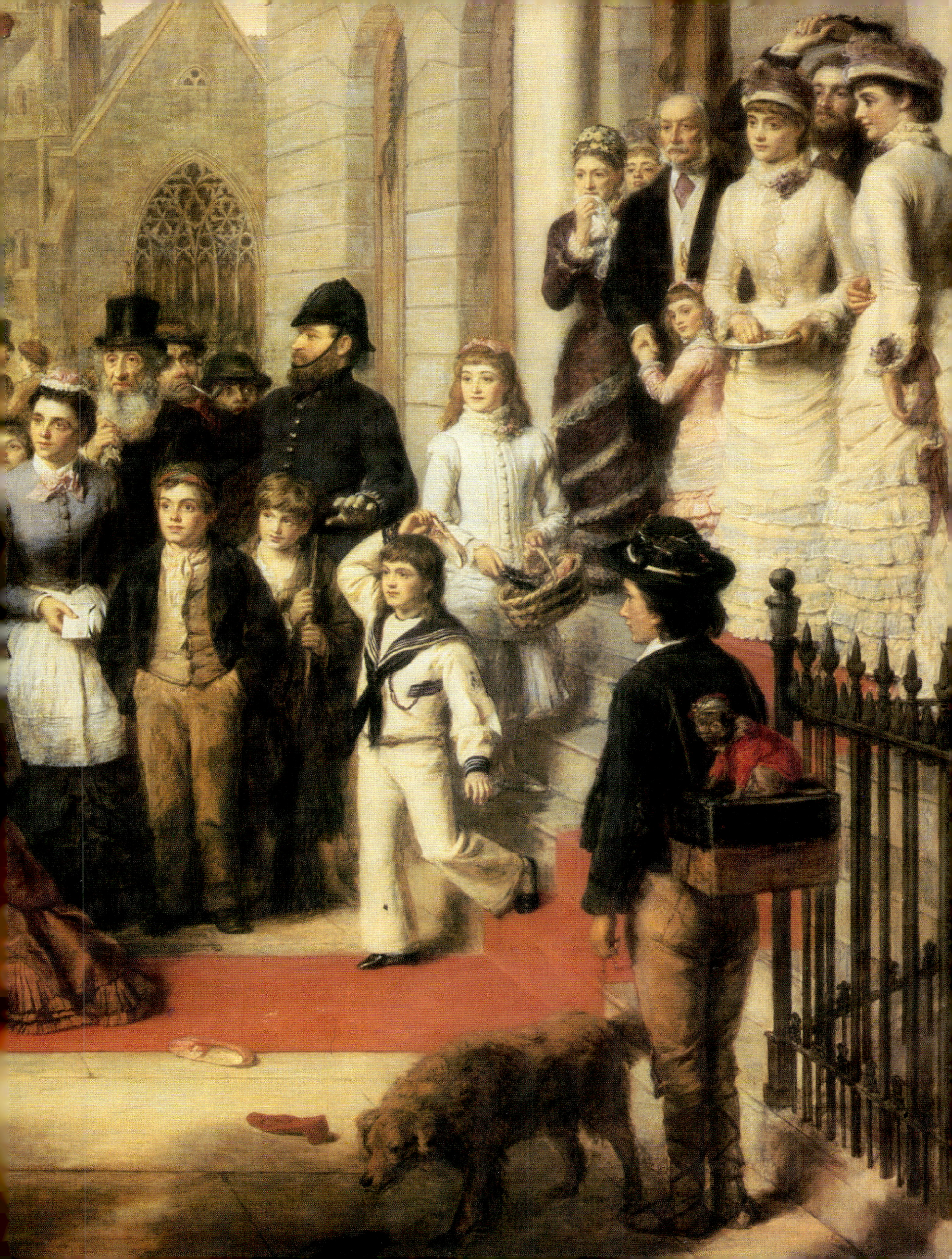

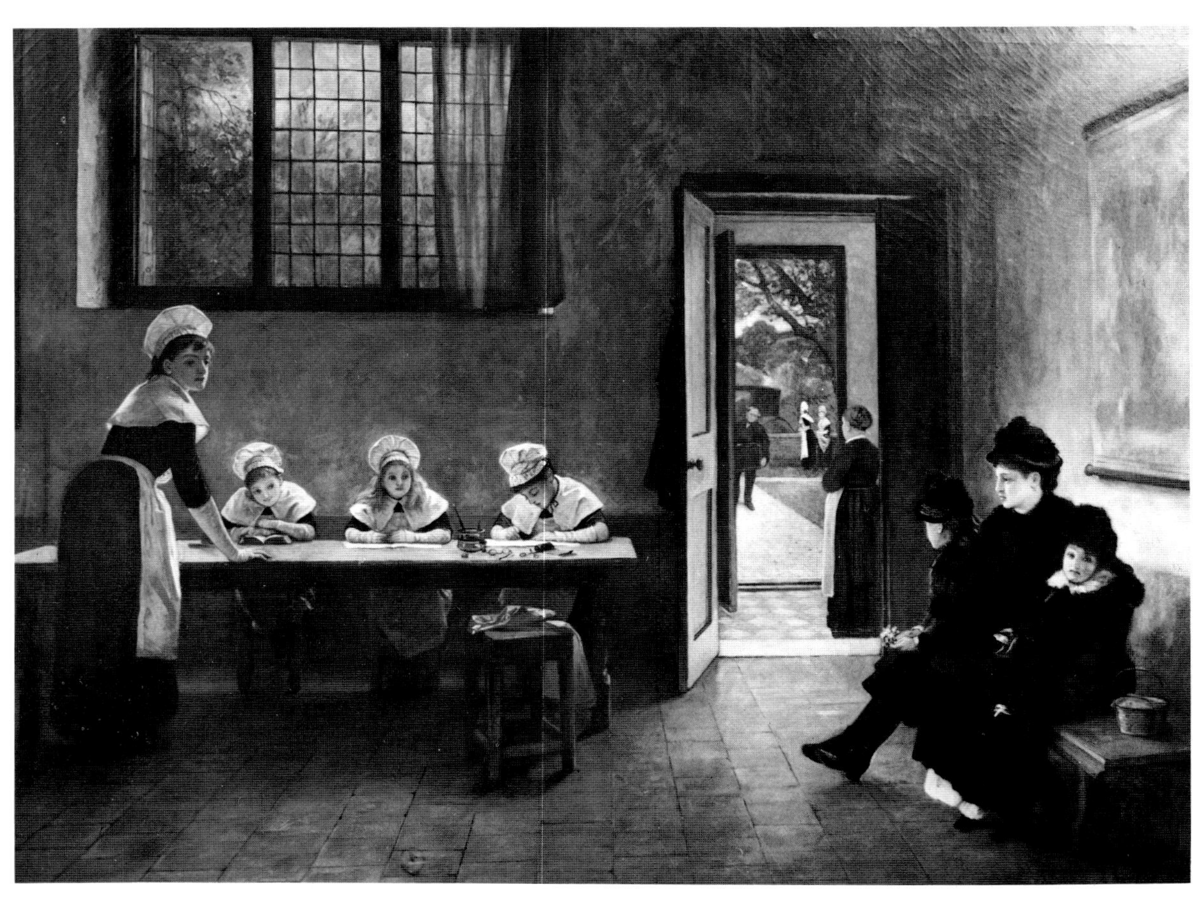

Plate 20

GEORGE ADOLPHUS STOREY (1834–1919)

*ORPHANS*, 1879

Oil on canvas, 39½ × 51½″

Another artist whose talent was apparent even in childhood, George Storey studied in Paris under Cabanel and Carolus-Duran during the late 1840s and early 1850s. From 1852 to 1854 he studied art in London where his first works exhibited at the Royal Academy were decidedly influenced by the Pre-Raphaelites. Thereafter, he contributed dozens of portraits and genre subjects to the Academy between 1851 and 1904, sending only a few to the Society of British Artists in the years between 1857 and 1880. A trip to Spain in 1862–1863 also seems to have had an impact on his art, especially since he copied various works by Velasquez there. Later he became affiliated with the St. John's Wood Clique, a group of artists that included Stacy Marks and William Yeames, among others. Some of Storey's works were compared with the earlier Dutch artist de Hoogh, whose palette and style of depicting figures in an interior, looking through an open doorway into the sunlight, are also evoked in *Orphans*.

*Orphans* was painted and exhibited in 1879, and it follows in the tradition of Storey's other works that indulged in somewhat sentimental depictions of females, including *The Bride's Burial*, 1859, *Sister*, 1869, *Mistress Dorothy*, 1873, *A Dancing Lesson*, 1876, and *Kept in School*. The subject of motherless and fatherless Victorian children was a favorite one, especially among writers, who could wring every tear out of the situation of a helpless and hapless young female in particular. While one critic described Storey's effort as aiming at mild pathos another, writing for *The Illustrated London News*, waggishly said, "Orphans! And who made them so? Oh, you Storey!" thus punning on the artist's name and his narrative intention in this picture. In terms of the story line, *The Art Journal* described it as "two sweet little girls in deep mourning . . . [being] ushered into the apartment which will be their future schoolroom; and three other little orphans, in the Asylum dress, look up from the desk and regard them with feelings of interest and sympathy."

The problem of homeless and destitute children was a very real one, especially in metropolitan areas, and Dr. Barnardo's first home for girls, for example, opened in London in 1873. Such institutions aimed at educating orphans and providing them with some industrial or vocational training, and many similar missions for such children were being founded throughout the country at this time. Later in the century more attention was given to providing sympathetic surrogate families for orphans, with cottage homes seen as alternatives to workhouses for both boy and girl inmates.

While the surroundings are austere in Storey's painting, they are not utterly grim; outside there are trees and areas for recreation, and inside the girls are being taught how to read, write, and sew. As is the case in Storey's picture, charity children were usually dressed in some sort of functional uniform; soon the young females at right will exchange their mourning attire for institutional garb, their other belongings to be relegated to the trunk that is being carried in for them.

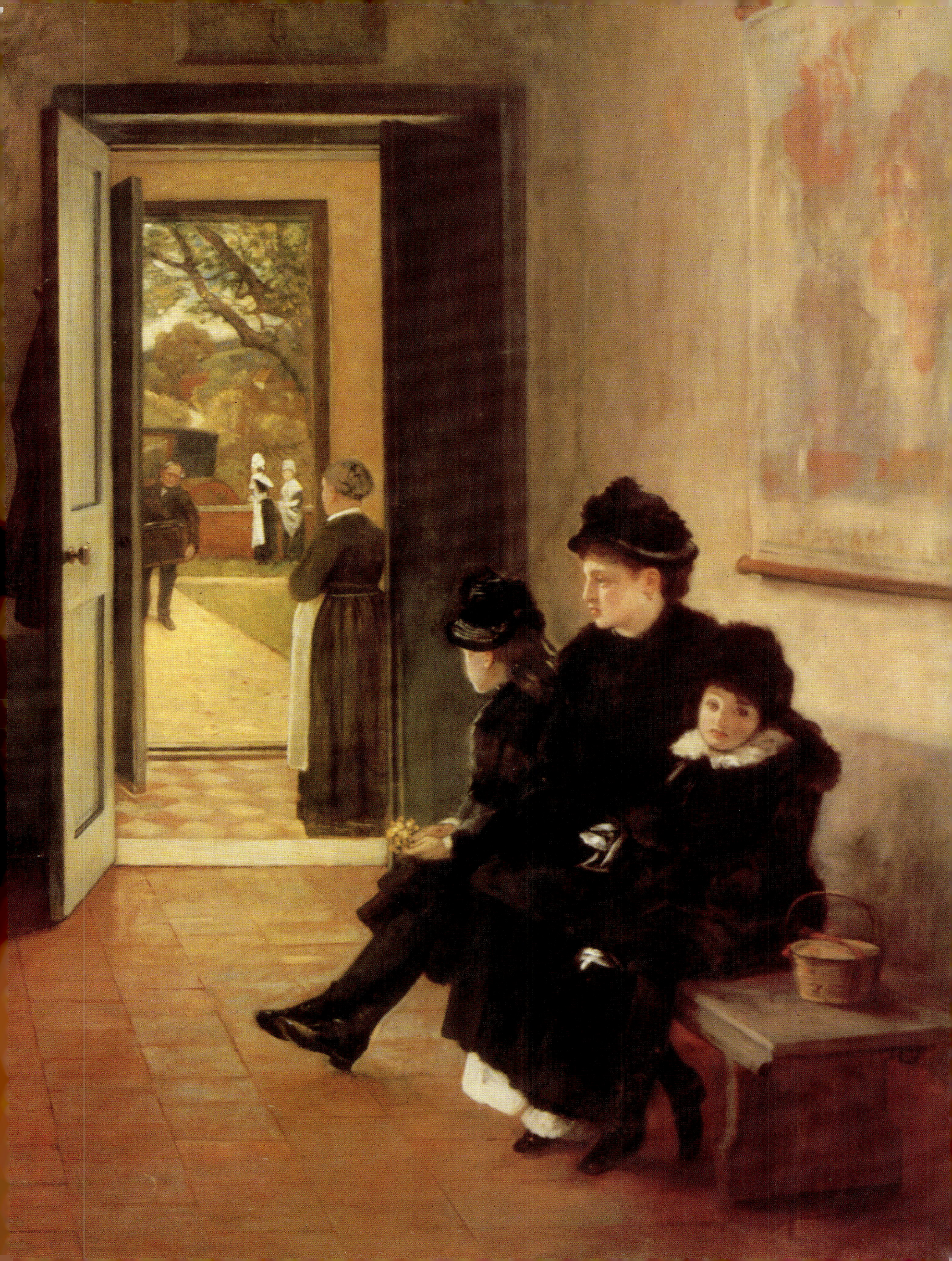

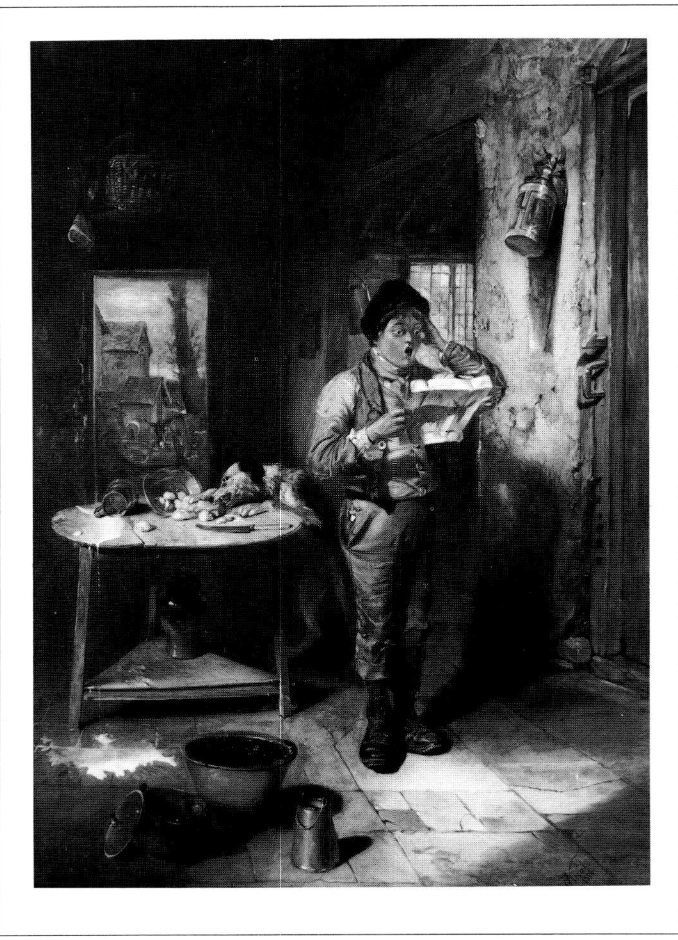

Plate 21

ERSKINE NICOL (1825–1904)

*THE "VALENTINE,"* 1874

Oil on canvas, 30 × 20¾″

Originally an apprentice to a housepainter in his native Edinburgh, Erskine Nicol in the first years of his career paradoxically made a reputation for painting amusing anecdotes of Irish life. Between 1851 and 1893 he exhibited numerous canvases at the Royal Academy, and a few of his pictures were also displayed and sold in America at the National Academy of Design and at the Philadelphia Centennial of 1876.

Most of Nicol's genre subjects are drawn from both Irish and Scottish peasant life and many have a humorous tone. Sometimes he repeats a particular motif or narrative pretext; for example, several pictures revolve around the arrival or reading of a letter or newspaper. Typically, the cottager is shown reacting with a rather exaggerated facial expression—grimacing or smiling as he or she struggles to read, sign a document, or compose a letter. Other artists also used the letter as a convenient story-telling device: it is an allusion to romance in Charles W. Cope's *Palpitation*, 1844, and the vehicle for transmitting news from abroad in James Collinson's *Answering the Emigrant's Letter*. Part of this preoccupation with getting or sending missives can be explained by the reform of the postal system of 1840, when the penny post was established and made delivery of mail both reliable and cheap. As a result, the valentine industry flourished in the 1840s and 1850s, when embossed, hand-punched, lace-trimmed, folded, and every other kind of sentimental or comic valentine flooded the market.

While Nicol painted another work entitled *The Valentine* in 1863, that picture shows a pretty peasant woman in a humble interior leisurely reading a message from an admirer. Although it was more customary for men to send valentines as a part of the courtship ritual than to receive them, here the message—a large drawing of a donkey—is a dubious compliment. Victorian valentines often were printed with quite funny—even scathing—verse, but there were also mass-produced declarations of intimacy that might cause a blush or surprised reaction.

The young boy in this painting, in his ragged clothes and oversized shoes, is clearly overwhelmed by the contents of his letter, and his face registers his astonishment as he sees the image of a mule on the treasured "valentine." Outside, a real mule or donkey can be glimpsed through the doorway, reinforcing the connotation of its stubborn or negative traits to both the boy and the viewer. The postmark on the letter appears to be the word "bray," yet another allusion to a donkey. Other objects in the painting may also project some emblematic meaning, especially if they were intended in the tradition of Nicolas Maes's seventeenth-century Dutch moralizing genre scenes. For example, is spilled milk a sign of the boy's general sloppiness or perhaps some reference to his possible neglect of a young lass? In addition, the dog clearly has an appetite for his master's goods and voraciously eats from the table; perhaps there is also some parallel to be drawn between this unmannerly animal and the boy. However much we read into this painting, Victorian viewers would undoubtedly have laughed at the boy's personal and romantic predicament.

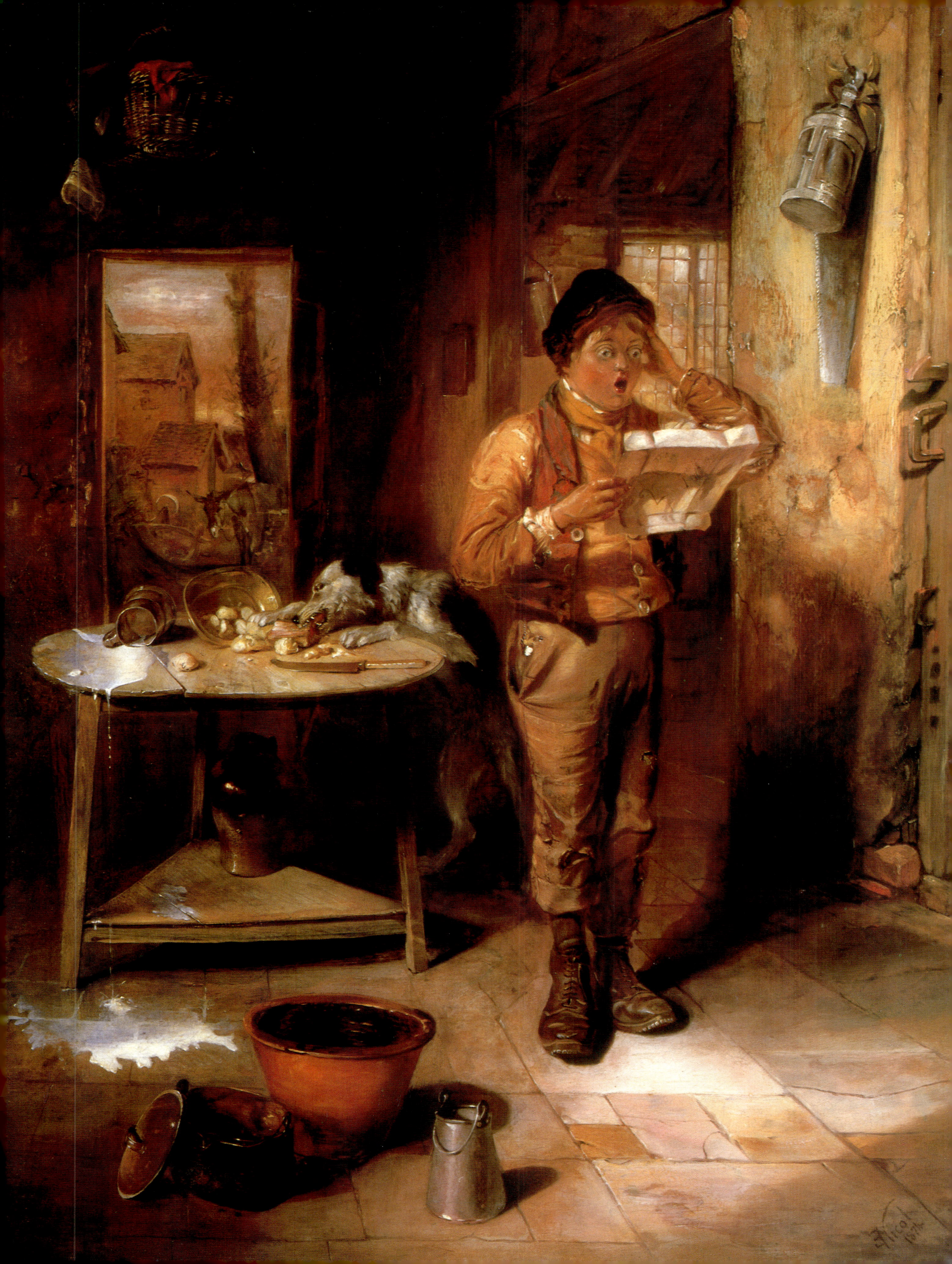

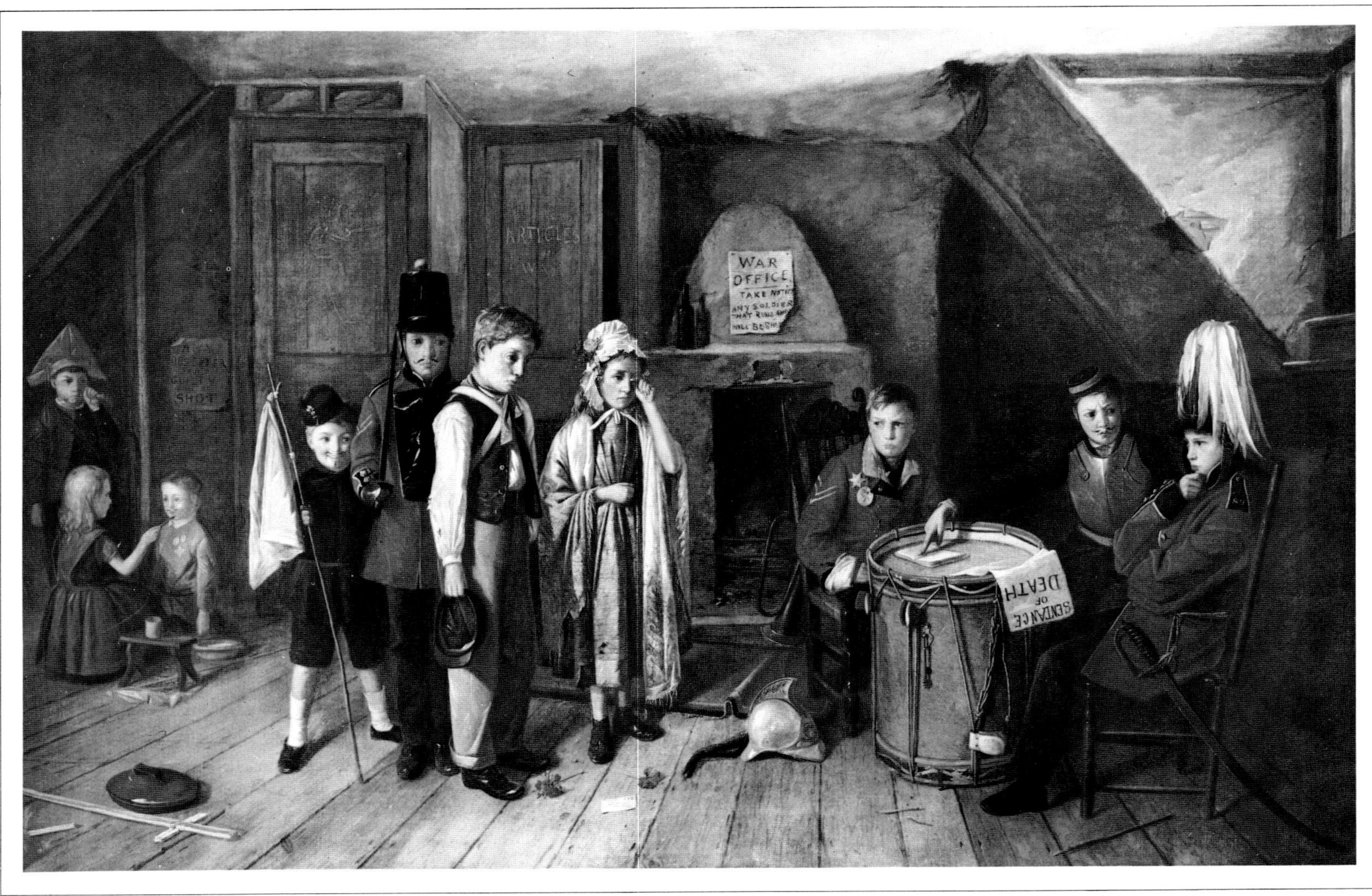


Plate 22

CHARLES HUNT (1803–1877)

*THE TRIBUNAL*, 1870

Oil on canvas, 29¼ × 44½″

A minor painter of amusing genre pictures, Charles Hunt exhibited at the Society of British Artists from 1846 until 1878 with such entries as *Boys Playing at Marbles*, 1848, and *The Dame's School*, 1868. He also exhibited briefly at the British Institution between 1858 and 1863 and sporadically at the Royal Academy between 1862 and 1891. Although it is not clear whether he was influenced directly by the Cranbrook Colony of artists, his work was sometimes compared to that of Thomas Webster because of the shared focus on children and their antics. In Hunt's case, high literature was often the source of his humorous parodies, and the first of these appeared in 1863 as a spoof of *Hamlet*. Later he varied his subject matter with trial scenes, *Trial by Judge and Jury*, 1866, and *The Trial Scene from "The Merchant of Venice,"* 1867, either of which may have been the inspiration for *The Tribunal*. This painting is also related to (or it may be the same as) an 1870 entry at the Royal Academy entitled *A Drum-Head Court Martial*.

Just as the Crimean War triggered a response from artists that brought forth a spate of rather patriotic pictures, so too were artists influenced by the Franco-Prussian War in 1870. (And in the years between these wars, military paintings still proliferated, as in Frederick Hardy's *The Volunteers* of 1860.) This is the underlying military inspiration for *The Tribunal*, although the subject is placed in the context of child's play here as the boys crudely mimic adult soldiers. A trio of lads at right serves as the tribunal, and each of their expressions—sternness, deliberation, disapproval—is exaggerated. Signs in the room indicate that this is the "War Office," with two notices proclaiming "any deserter found guilty will be shot," and "Take notice any soldier that runs away will be shot." The doors are scratched with drawings and writing, the "articles of war" inscription presumably related to the "sentence of death" contemplated by the tribunal as part of their policy for dealing with desertion.

While the subject of a soldier's desertion appeared in more serious guise in Richard Redgrave's *The Deserter's Home*, 1847, here a solemn matter is amusingly satirized by the role-playing of girls and boys. Escorted by two soldiers with painted mustaches, the abject "guilty party" has also brought along his weeping wife to plead on his behalf, much as family members might have accompanied real deserters in an attempt to receive mercy from the judges.

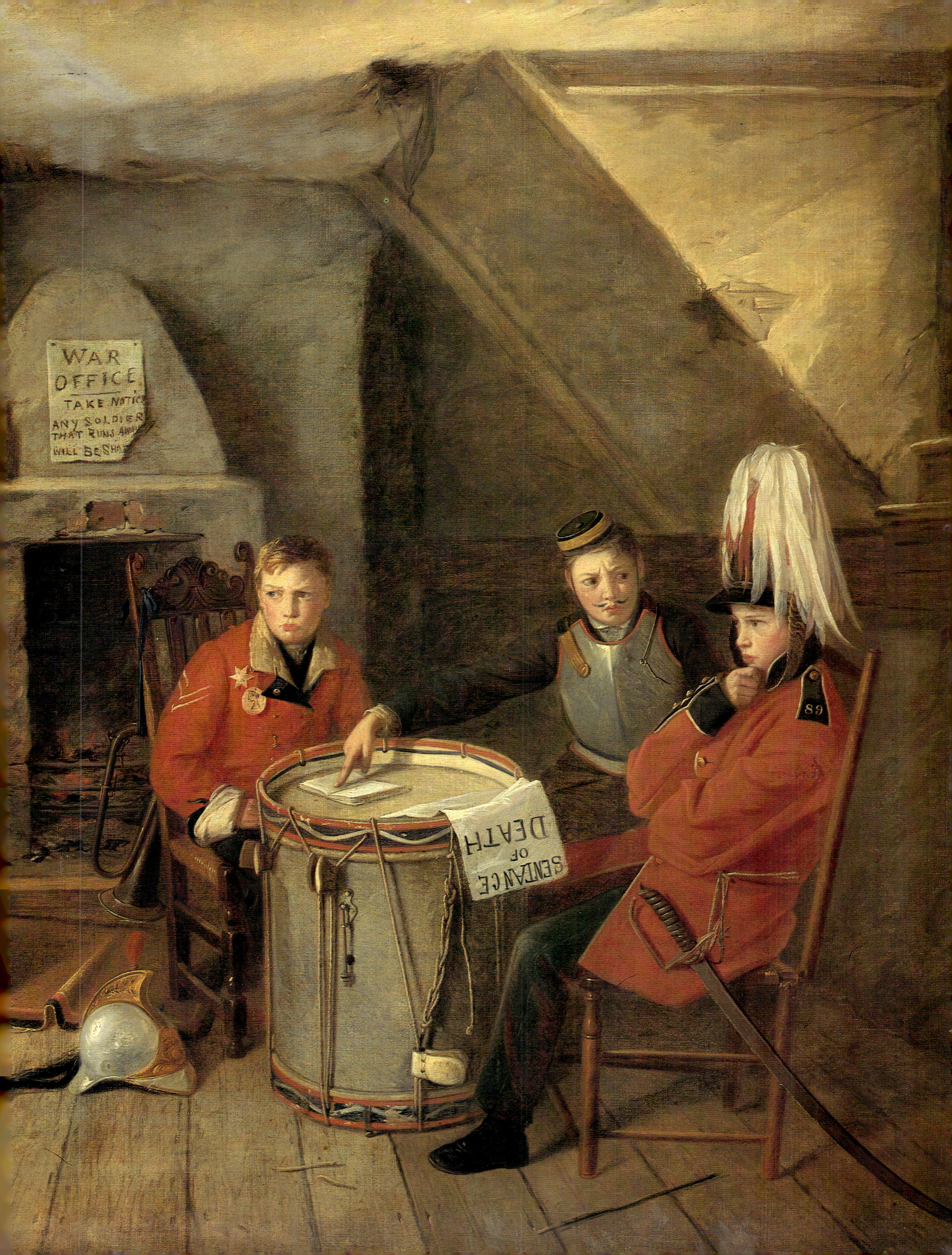
WAR
OFFICE
TAKE NOTIC
ANY SOLDIER
THAT RUNS AWA
WILL BE SHA
SENTANCE
OF
DEATH
89

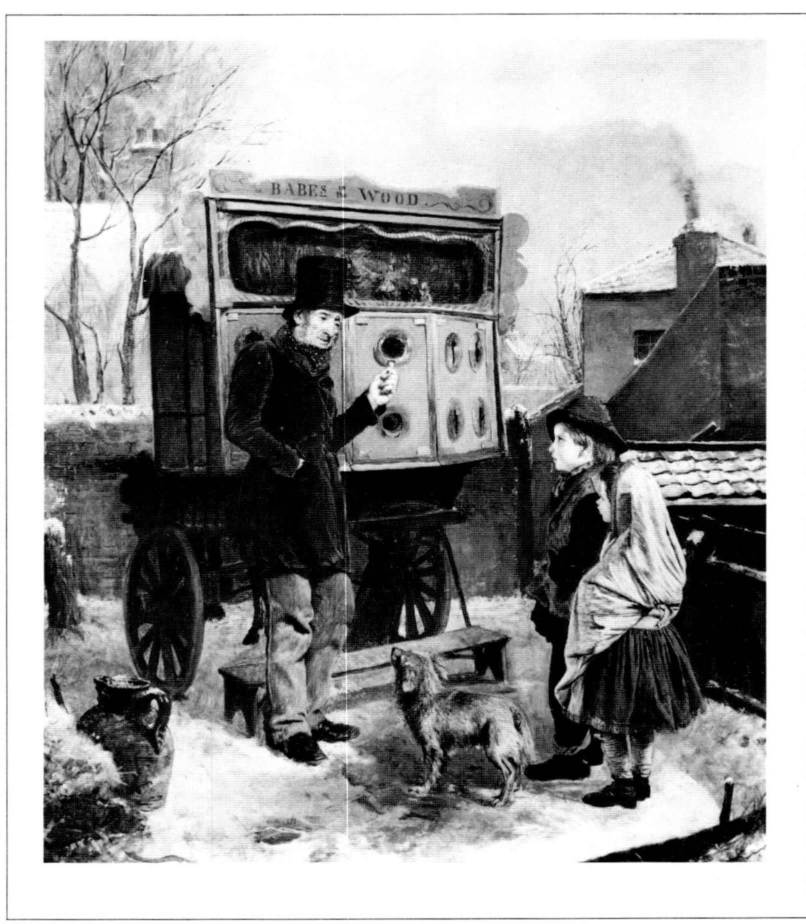


Plate 23

JOHN P. BURR (1834–1893)

*THE PEEPSHOW*, 1849

Oil on canvas, 40 × 33½″

After initial study in Edinburgh with his artist brother Alexander, John Burr exhibited numerous works such as *Preparing Dinner*, 1855, and *The Housewife*, 1858, at the Royal Scottish Academy before moving to London in 1861. Drawing upon the inspiration of David Wilkie, Robert Scott Lauder, and others, he focused on mostly Scottish genre subjects as well as the poems of Robert Burns. In his celebration of Scottish pastoral life he also produced many domestic scenes with children, including *Grandfather's Return*, *Children of the Sea*, *A Watercress Boy*, *A Market Girl*, and *The School House*. An active member of the Royal Society of British Artists and the Old Water-Colour Society, Burr also contributed intermittently to the Royal Academy from 1862 to 1882.

*The Peepshow* is one of at least two treatments of this theme by the artist, for a later work with the same title was exhibited at the Royal Academy in 1864. This was apparently a humorous depiction of an itinerant toy theater performer in a village street, and the comments of *The Athenaeum's* critic suggest a somewhat different composition: "See the fun of the child who carries the jug of beer and longs to stop, and the cleverly-put point of character in the young nurse who, restrained from her own curiosity, holds up her baby-charge to look through one of the spy-holes of the theater; see also the figures of the butcher's boy, who stands near the front of the picture, and of his companions who gather around." Here, however, there are only two children who, with their faithful dog, stand on the trampled snow to watch the peepshow. The arrival of such traveling showmen generated considerable excitement for the young, and Henry Mayhew in *London Labour and the London Poor* of 1861 interviewed one such performer and reported that, in good weather, he might earn at least three or four shillings per day and that this money was taken "more from children than grown people in London, and more from grown people than children in the country." Mayhew also mentioned that handicapped men often took up this occupation, since the equipment needed for exhibiting such small pictures was minimal and portable. (The actual apparatus was a box with a magnifying lens and apertures through which audiences could peep in order to see shifting miniature panoramas.)

Apparently certain subjects such as battles, murders, and historic moments were especially popular with both adults and the young, and these included the Death of Nelson, the Forty Thieves, and Queen Victoria Embarking for Scotland. In this painting the topic is "Babes in the Wood," a tale based on an English ballad about a greedy uncle who wants to have two children taken to the woods to be killed. This rather sensational story was popular both in the operatic and literary traditions, and between 1800 and 1870 scores of illustrations of the tale appeared, including Lady Waterford's 1849 edition of *The Babes in the Wood*. Of course, the children seen here are themselves "babes in the wood," presumably being still inexperienced in the ways of the world.

Thomas Webster also painted a peepshow scene of the Battle of Waterloo in 1864, while Punch and Judy were treated by Arthur Boyd Houghton and Charles Hunt, among others. Peep shows were the subjects of *Watching the Show* and *Watching Jack the Giant Killer*, both painted in 1857 by Matthias Robinson. They depicted amused members of the audience reacting to the saga unfolding behind the spy-holes.

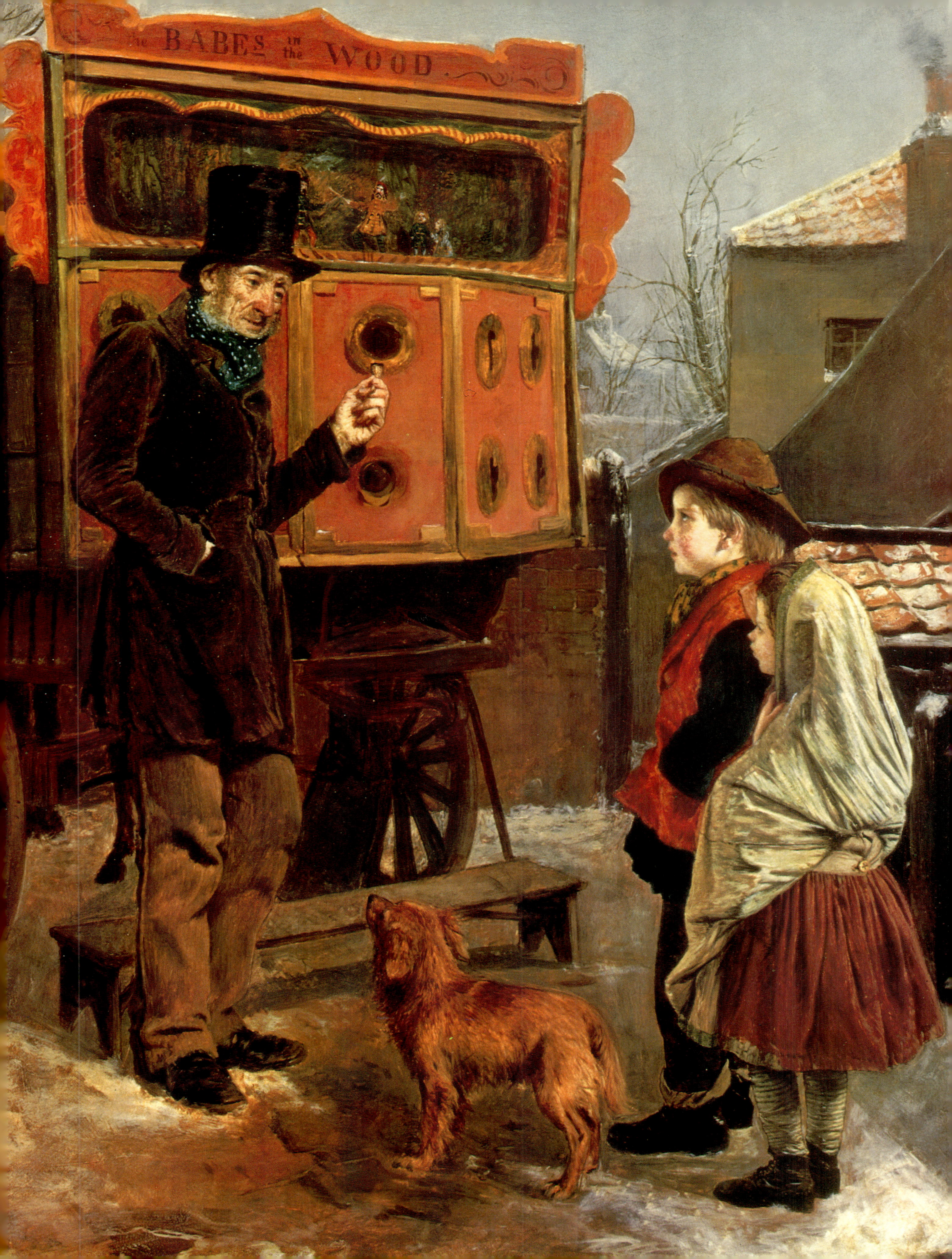
BABES in the WOOD

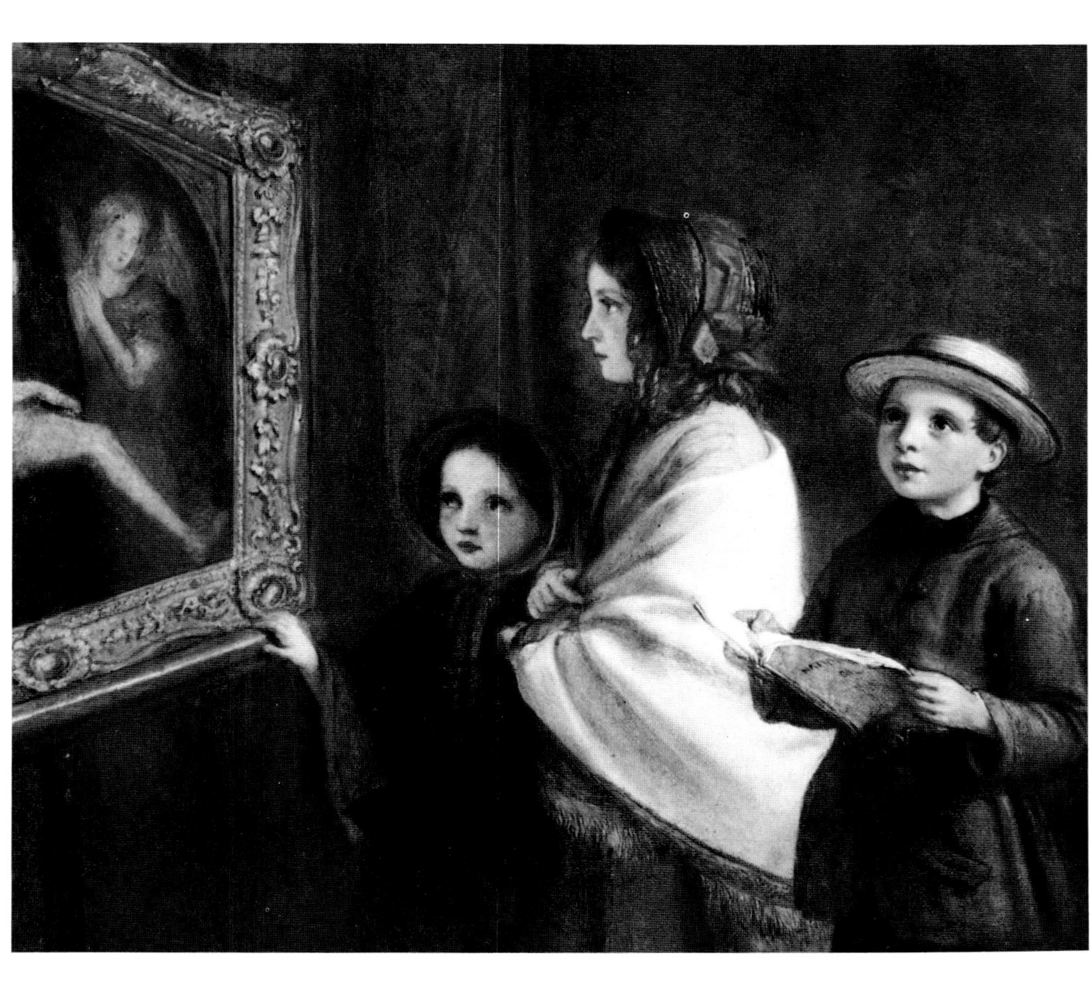

Plate 24

CHARLES COMPTON (fl. 1847–67)

*A STUDY IN THE NATIONAL GALLERY*, 1855

Oil on canvas, 10 × 12¼″

Few biographical details are known about Charles Compton, who seems to have been acquainted with some of the Pre-Raphaelite artists and admired Millais's paintings in particular. Compton exhibited at the Royal Academy between 1847 and 1857 and won a silver medal for one of his compositions, contributing on a more sporadic basis to the Society of British Artists between 1849 and 1867.

Some of his subjects were literary in origin, such as his illustration of a passage from Izzak Walton's *Life of Richard Hooker*, and others treated the theme of childhood, as in *The Sick Child*, 1847, and *A Young Student* painted three years later. A few canvases explored the idea of the young creative genius, the subject of his 1849 Royal Academy entry about seven-year-old Benjamin West's early art, as well as of his *Young Sculptor's First Effort*, 1849.

*A Study in the National Gallery* examines the reactions of three young connoisseurs of fine art, the precocity of the viewers reinforced by their sustained and even pious interest in the religious picture on the wall. The boy holds a guidebook to the National Gallery and looks up at a *Pietà* which is identifiable as part of a lunette by Francesco Francia, purchased by the museum in 1841. Attending art exhibitions, especially at the Royal Academy, was a favorite public activity, and while sometimes only one connoisseur is depicted (as in Gustave Pope's 1862 *Academy View* with its pretty female visitor), many Victorian paintings of this subject include a cross section of the social classes. While the crowd of art-lovers in George Bernard O'Neill's 1863 *Public Opinion* and Thomas Hall's 1867 *One Touch of Nature Makes the Whole World Kin* seems both well-fed and enthusiastic, a decidedly ominous undertone is struck in John Leech's 1843 *Punch* cartoon entitled "Substance and Shadow." In the latter the hungry and handicapped poor are contrasted with the portraits of aristocrats on the walls and the reality of middle- and upper-class spectators who seem scornful of the "interlopers." The child artist or viewer is one aspect of this theme, the object of pity in William MacDuff 's 1852 *Shaftesbury, or Lost and Found* (where two ragged shoeblacks peer into a printshop window to admire a portrait of the social reformer Lord Shaftesbury) and the object of mild humor in Charles Hunt's *In the Museum* of 1870.

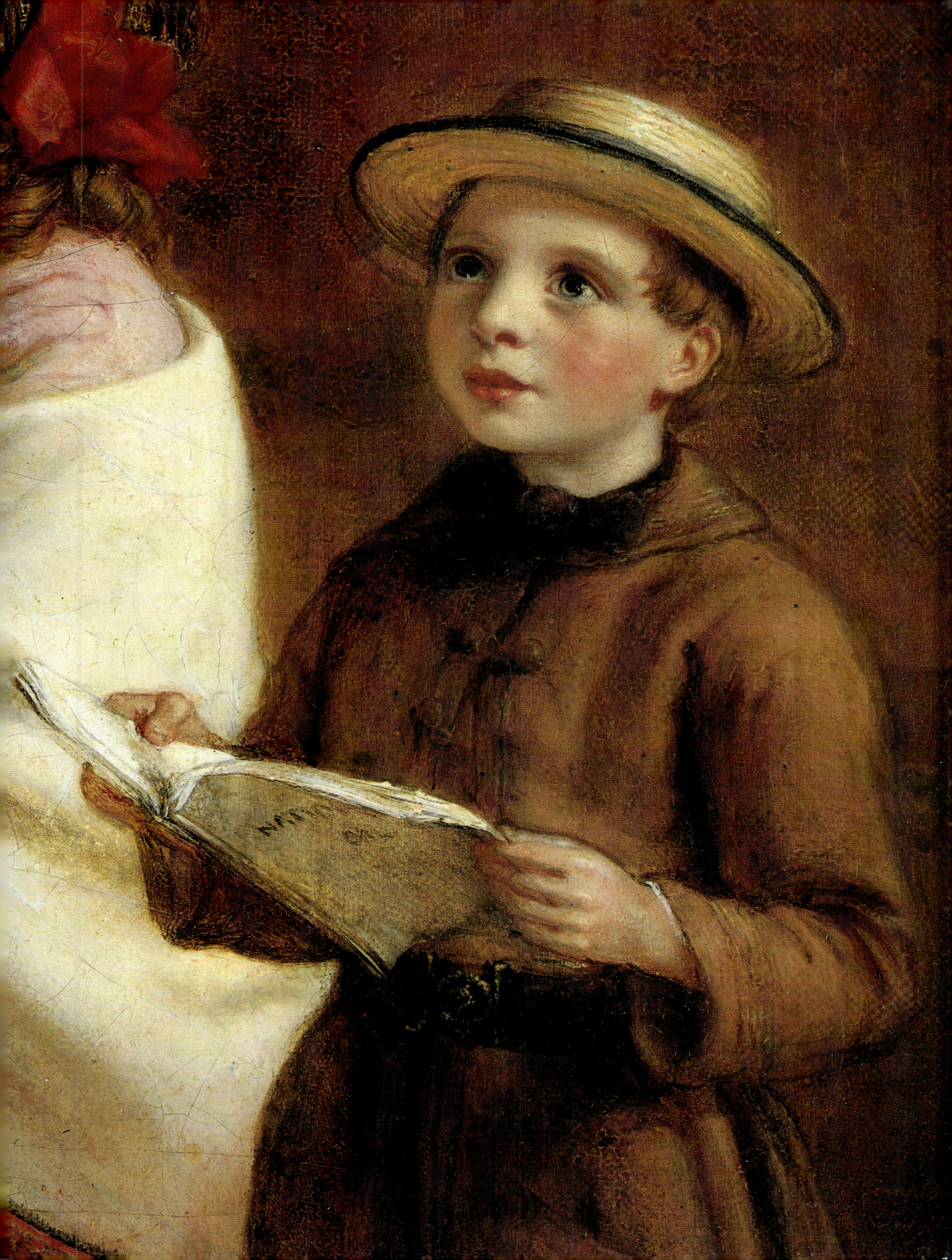

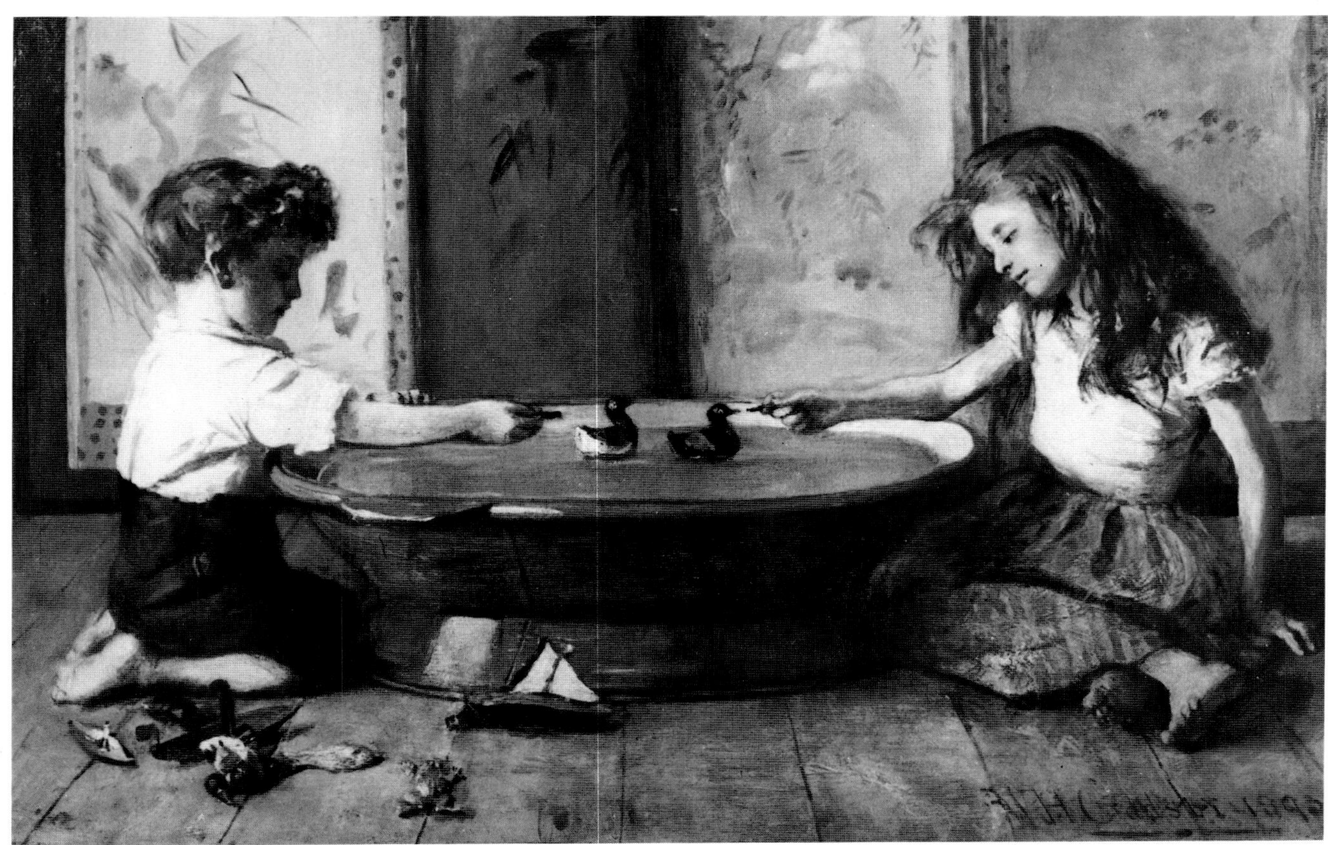

Plate 25
WILLIAM GADSBY (fl. 1869–94)
*CHILDREN PLAYING IN A HIP-BATH*, 1893
Oil on canvas, 21 × 33½″

Few biographical details are known about William Gadsby, who exhibited several dozen works, primarily at the Royal Society of British Artists, between 1871 and 1894, and sporadically at the Royal Academy. Many of his pictures had titles which indicate that children at play were a preferred subject.

In this canvas, a young boy and girl play together at a hip-bath, each holding a magnet with which to maneuver the metal toy ducks afloat in a miniature ocean. While barefoot and casually dressed, the children are probably affluent, since they play near an expensive *japoniste* screen. Gadsby also dealt with related themes in *The Lessening Sail*, 1872, and *After the Bath*, 1893–4. Maritime toy craft and submarines—steam-powered, mechanically driven, or otherwise—were very popular with Victorian and Edwardian youngsters, and an entire industry developed to accommodate the middle-class market for such playthings.

Plate 26
CHARLES HODGE MACKIE (1862–1920)
*THE JAPANESE DOLL*, ca. 1900–10
Oil on canvas, 19½ × 18″

Charles Mackie was a Scottish painter whose first works were exhibited in the 1880s in Edinburgh; he subsequently sent paintings to the Royal Academy, the Royal Society of Artists, and the Royal Hibernian Academy.

*The Japanese Doll* is one of a number of Mackie's figural compositions that portrayed children, as in *The Skipping Rope*, 1901. From the 1880s onwards there was a spate of pictures showing children in "aesthetic" dress and surroundings, and this work by Mackie seems to fit in this category. A well-dressed young girl lounges rather prettily amid pillows and a patterned (possibly Navaho or other exotic type) rug, her focus of attention a Japanese doll puppet. Oriental dolls had become popular in Europe after the 1855 exposition in Paris, and in the 1890s they were often dressed to look like contemporary Japanese children or adults. During the Russo-Japanese war in 1904–5, these playthings were even more in demand, and both German and Japanese manufacturers produced them for commercial export.

Plate 27
WILLIAM HOLMAN HUNT (1827–1919)
*MRS. WILSON AND HER CHILD*, 1851–3
Oil on canvas, 14 × 18″

One of the founders of the Pre-Raphaelite Brotherhood, William Holman Hunt was also the only one of the group to remain true to the creed and stylistic exactitude of the first phase of Pre-Raphaelitism. In the 1850s Hunt produced some of his best work, including *The Hireling Shepherd*, 1852, and *The Awakening Conscience*, 1854.

Hunt had three sisters, one of whom—Emily—also became an art student. Sarah Hunt Wilson, born in 1829, was apparently supportive of her brother's artistic goals in his youth, and she may have later advised him on his relationship with the somewhat dubious young model named Annie Miller. Among Hunt's many portraits in various media were those of important women in his life. In this unfinished canvas, he casts his sister Sarah in a traditional role as a young mother, depicting her with the first of several children that she bore. In later years the relationship between Hunt and Sarah became estranged, the artist complaining to a friend about his bankrupt brother-in-law's "stupidity and indifference; the father of little Teddy has too many children for me to think of supporting."

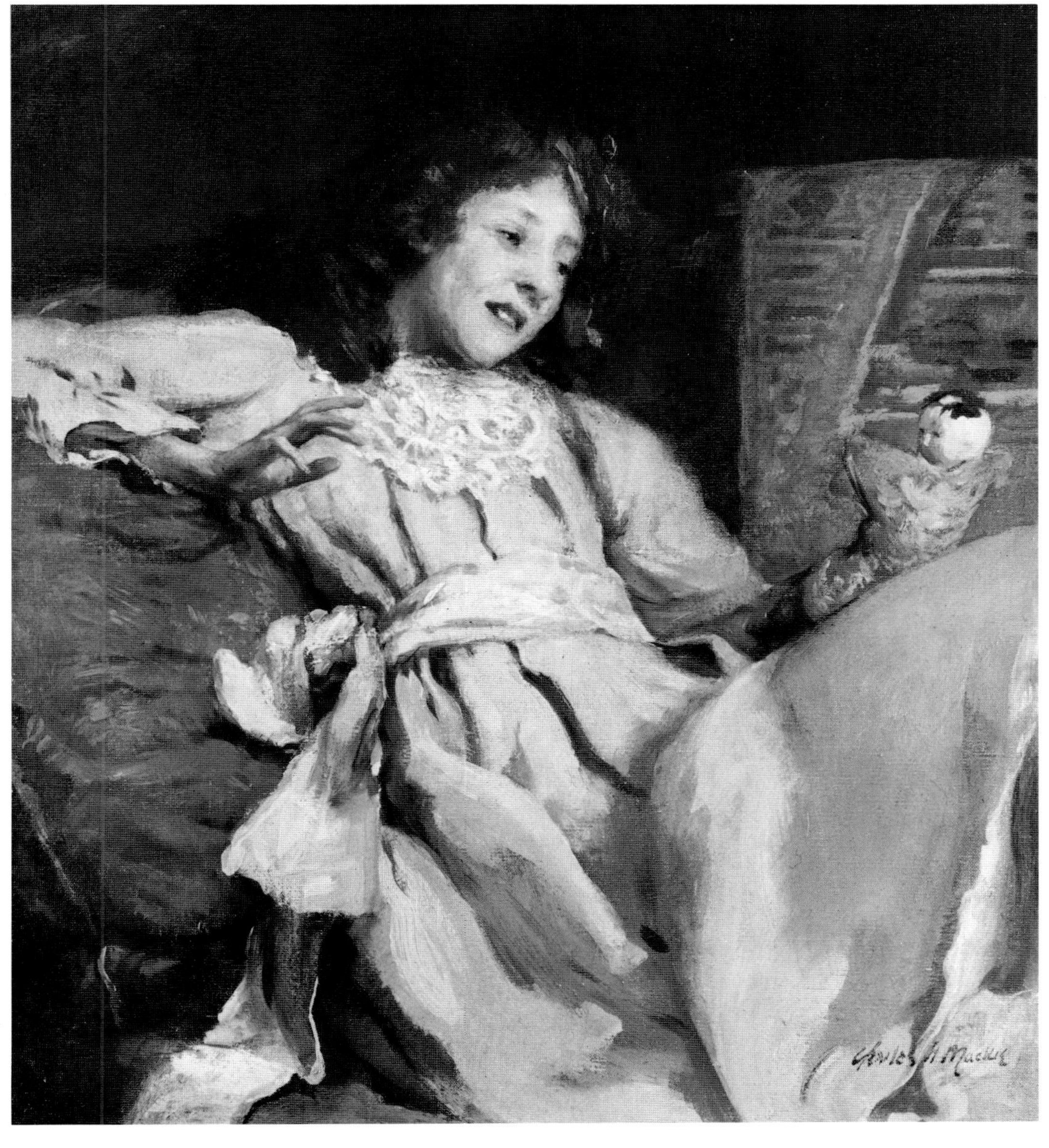

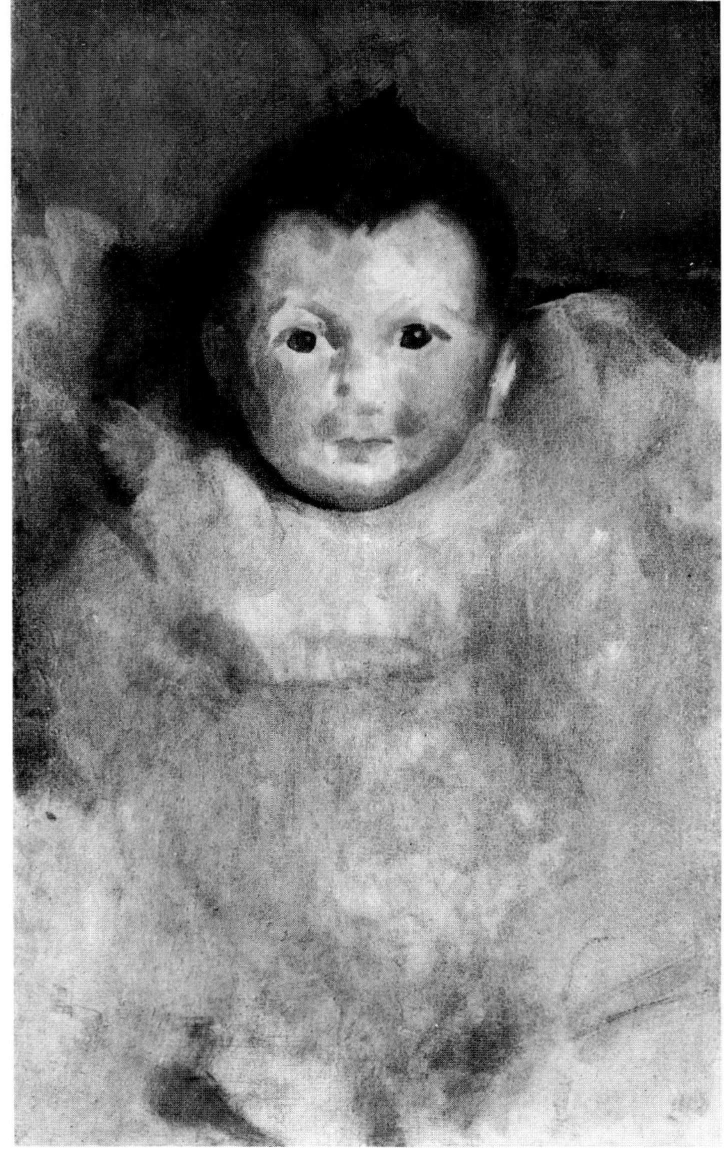

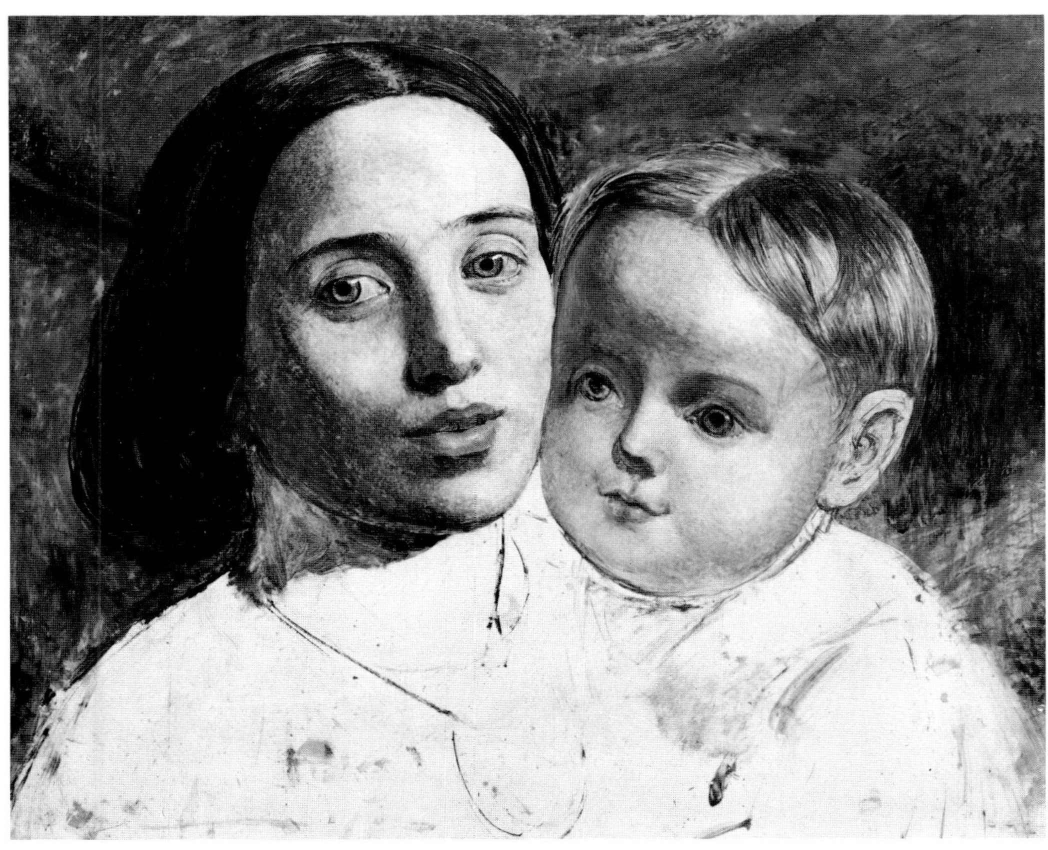

Plate 28

JAMES ABBOTT McNEILL WHISTLER

(1834–1903)

*PORTRAIT OF*
*MISS AMY BRANDON THOMAS,*
1890

Oil on canvas, 19½ × 11½″

The American-born James Whistler was one of the most cosmopolitan and eminent of nineteenth-century artists, having worked both in London and in Paris at various times in his career. Some of his most beautiful and aesthetic portraits had been of girls, and the infant in this canvas was Amy Thomas, the daughter of a playwright who greatly admired Whistler's work. Brandon Thomas and his wife also appeared in an 1891 lithograph, but here their offspring (who initially posed at age six months) is the focus of attention. Apparently the artist asked Mrs. Thomas to bring the child to him again several months after the portrait had been started and was quite dismayed that his sitter had so altered in appearance. Whistler allegedly told his friend he instead wanted "the one he had before" and sent the parent and child home. This accounts for the unfinished nature of the portrait, which nonetheless reveals some of Whistler's working methods and fluid style as well as the way he had begun to capture an alert and candid expression in the baby's face.

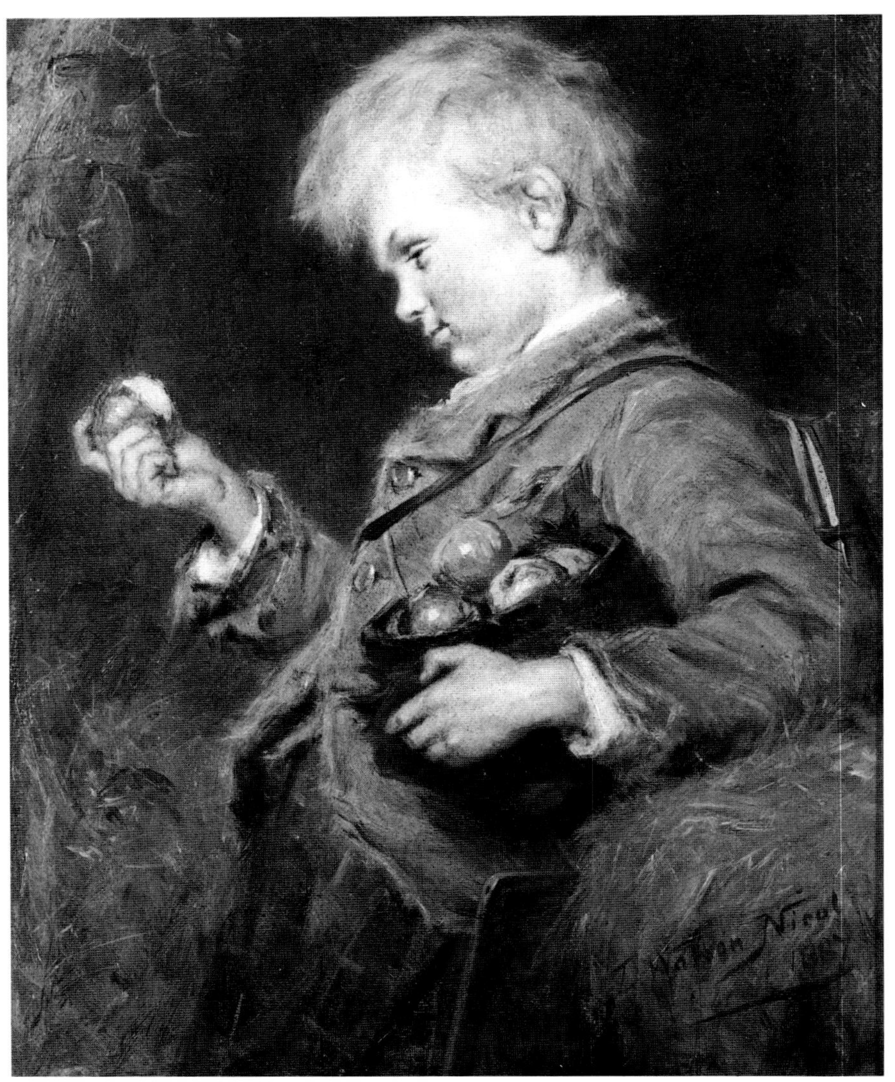

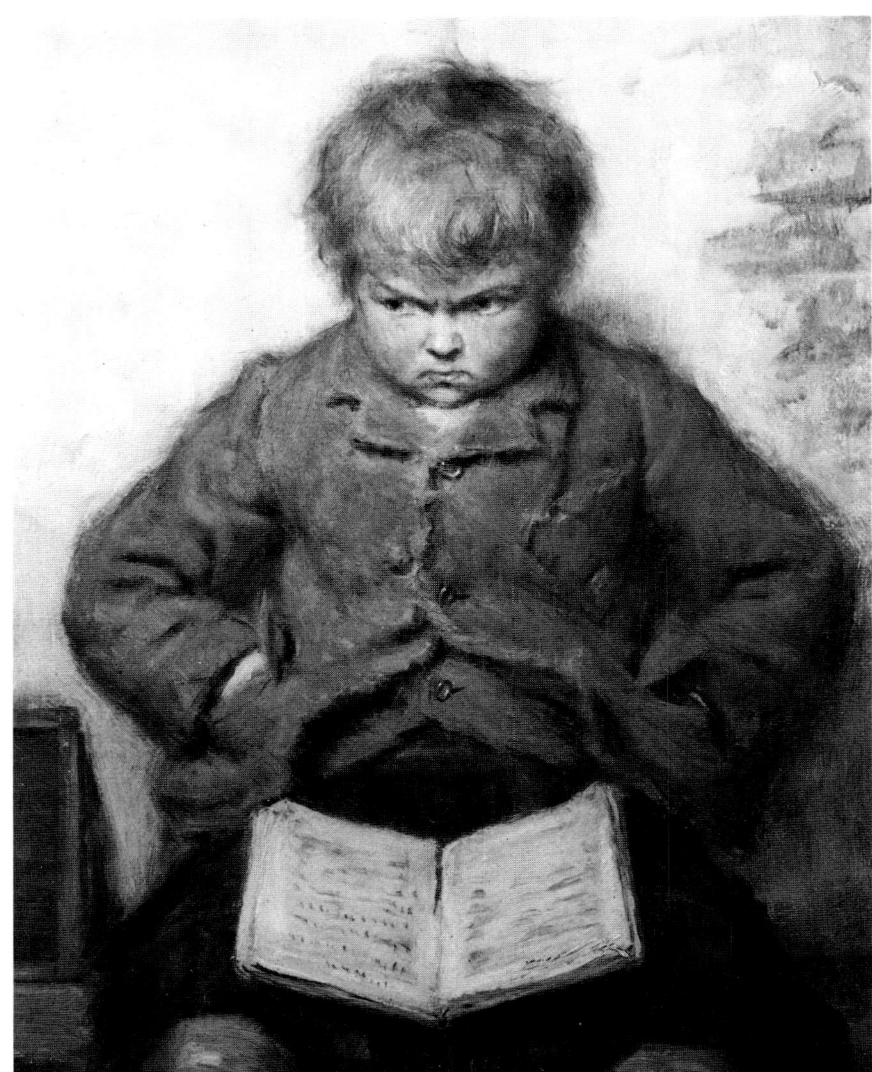

Plate 29–30

JOHN WATSON NICOL (fl. 1876–1924)

CAUSE and EFFECT, 1887

Both, oil on canvas, 10½ × 8″

The son of a Scottish artist of the same name, John Watson Nicol exhibited numerous paintings inspired by literary, religious, and historical subjects at the Royal Academy between 1876 and 1924. Genre pictures with childhood as the focus were not typical of his works, however. *Cause* and *Effect* follow in the tradition of Edwin Landseer's images of children and especially those of Thomas Webster, particularly the latter's 1841 picture entitled *The Frown*. Serial pictures were popular with viewers, and these two single-figure compositions chronicle a young boy's mischievousness and its consequences. A lad in a tartan kilt with a strapload of books on his back holds a basketful of apples and rather slyly eats one of them in *Cause*. It is unclear whether he is being punished for eating in class, for taking the teacher's apple, or for another infraction in *Effect*, the pendant in which the boy is now quite dour and angry as he sits with an open book.

Plate 31

CHARLES HUNT (1803–1877)

IVANHOE, 1871

Oil on canvas, 29¼ × 44⅜″

Charles Hunt produced myriad canvases in which children put on costumes or disguises to stage amateur theatricals based on literary sources. Here Sir Walter Scott's famous novel—a tale of romantic conflict, rivalry, and royal battles—is the source of inspiration. In the great tournament at Ashby-de-la-Zouche, at which Ivanhoe defeats everyone in his adversary's camp, he must also contend with a knight named Sir Brian de Bois-Guilbert, whose name is painted on the armor of the nearly overthrown figure at right. The children have apparently been reading *Ivanhoe* and while the two lads at right hold the book, the others try to pantomime it. The noble Ivanhoe lunges at an opponent from his imaginary steed, while court of female onlookers—including his beloved Rowena—encourages him, and at the far left another character has his makeup applied so he can join this world of make-believe.

As is typical in such pantomime/parody canvases by Hunt, the setting is an attic chamber where children and their imaginations can rule supreme, and adult interlopers rarely intervene.

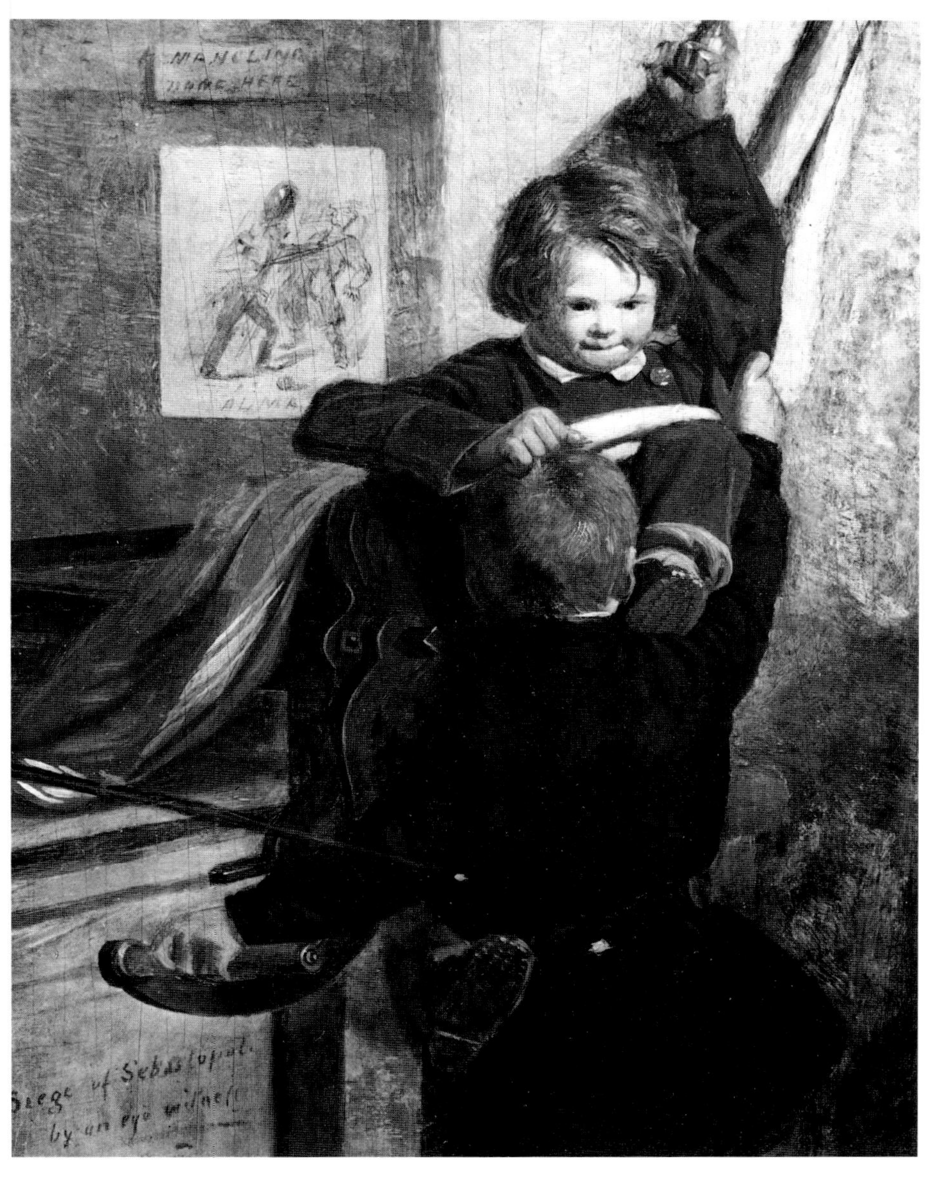


Plate 32

JAMES COLLINSON (1825–1881)

*THE SIEGE OF SEBASTOPOL, BY AN EYEWITNESS*, 1856

Oil on canvas, 10½ × 8¼"

One of the original members of the Pre-Raphaelite Brotherhood, James Collinson first attracted the attention of Dante Gabriel Rossetti in 1847 with a Royal Academy entry entitled *The Charity Boy's Debut*. Various later pictures focused on boyish exploits; however, this painting is less about child's play than it is a treatment of the contemporary theme of the Crimean war. Other artists such as John Everett Millais and Jerry Barrett had dealt with this topic, as did Collinson himself in a lost work of 1856 entitled *A Crimean Hero* and *Home Again* of the following year.

In *The Siege of Sebastopol*, two boys engage in make-believe combat, while in a sketch (inscribed "Alma") on the wall a soldier lunges at an adversary. The title of the picture derives from an important 1854 campaign in the Crimea, in which English soldiers defeated the Russians at Alma and elsewhere but could not eject them for many months from Sebastopol. Collinson himself never traveled to the Crimea but, like his young protagonists, is reacting to the Victorian hero worship and fantasies of bloodless war.

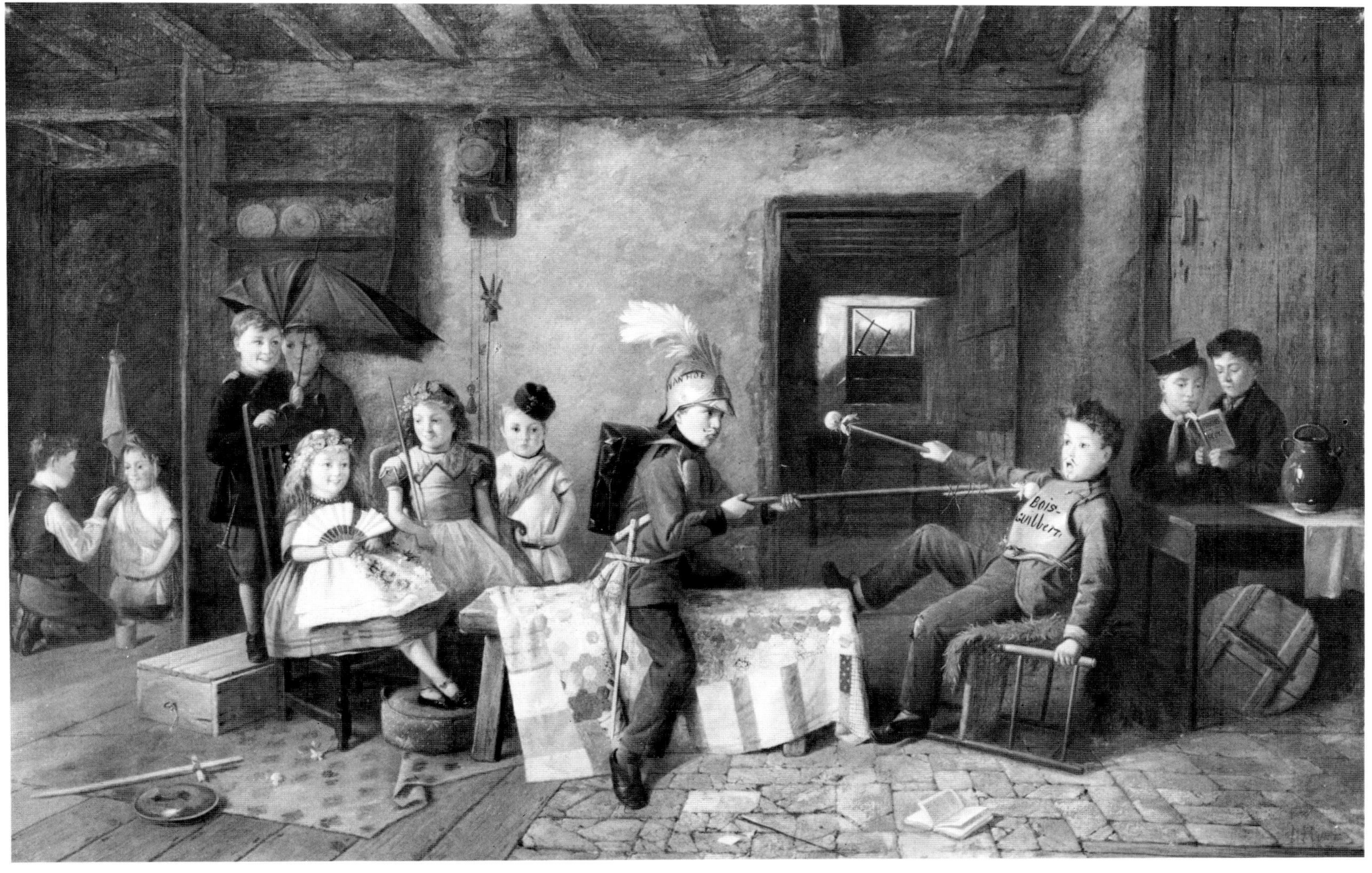

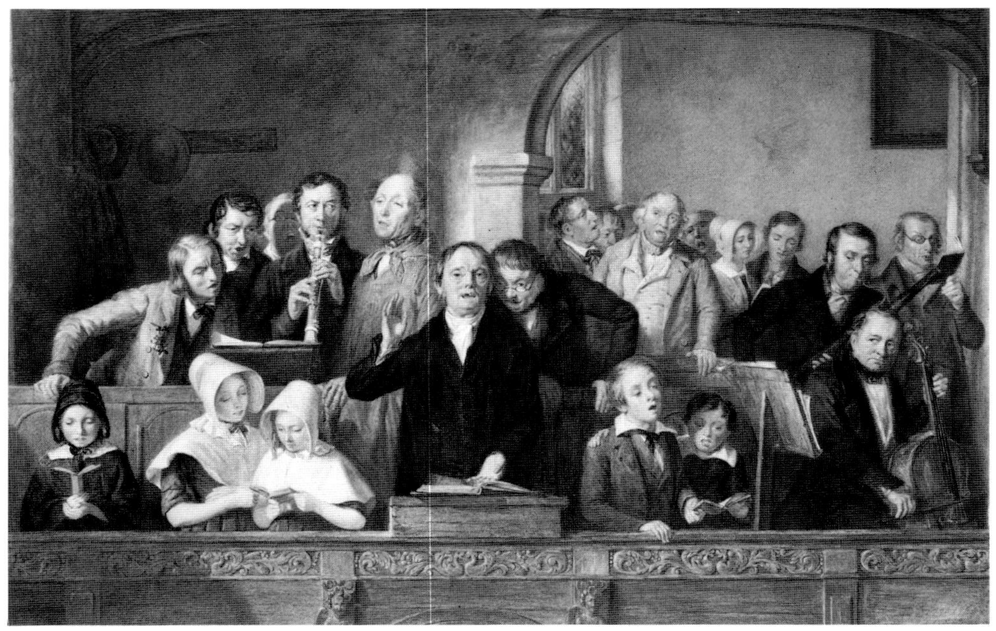

Plate 33
THOMAS WEBSTER (1800–1886)
*A VILLAGE CHOIR*, ca. 1847
Watercolor, 22½ × 34½″

The son of a member of the Royal Household, Thomas Webster was educated in the Choir of St. George's Chapel, Windsor and the Chapel Royal in St. James's. A musical career may have awaited, but instead Webster began training as an artist at the Royal Academy in 1821 and within a few years scored success with the public.

The original large oil version of *A Village Choir* was commissioned by John Sheepshanks, whose important collection is now at the Victoria & Albert Museum. The source was an excerpt from Washington Irving's *Sketch Book* describing a scene in which a country choir of amateur musicians and singers performs in church. Irving called them "country bumpkins" and *The Art Journal* described the characters in the painting as "about as motley an assemblage of choristers as can well be imagined." Around the toothless choral leader are a discordant group of players and vocalizers, all of these producing a clearly cacophonous effect.

Plate 34
PAUL FALCONER POOLE (1807–1879)
*THE EMIGRANT'S DEPARTURE*, ca. 1838
Oil on panel, 26 × 36″

Paul Falconer Poole was largely self-taught, but he went on to achieve considerable success, exhibiting literary, genre, and biblical subjects at the Royal Academy especially between 1830 and 1879. Relatively few of his pictures seem to have treated contemporary political or social problems, but *The Emigrant's Departure* was one of the first of a stream of emigration pictures that dealt with the increasing exodus of working people from the British Isles. This painting seems to be the one exhibited at the Royal Academy in 1838 and accompanied by the following lines from Oliver Goldsmith's eighteenth-century poem, "The Deserted Village": "What sorrows gloomed that parting day,/That called them from their native land away." In this scene of leavetaking the children also participate, embracing one another for the last time and also symbolizing the link between generations and between the past and the present.

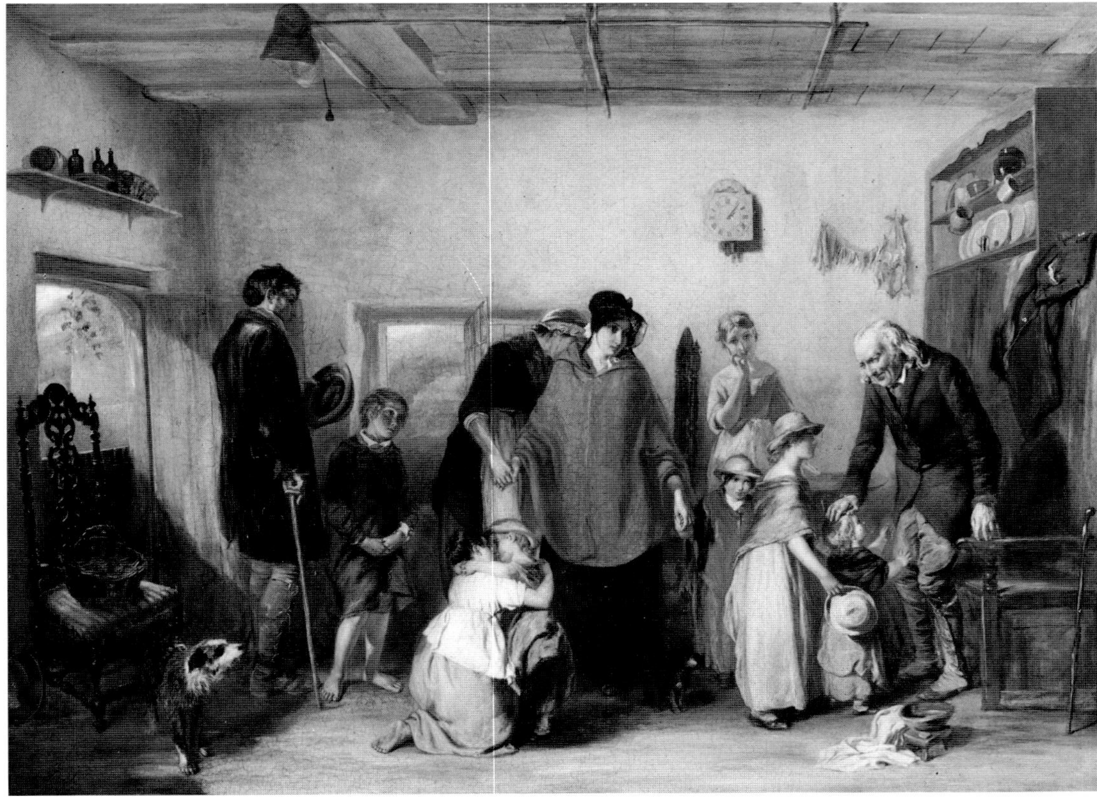

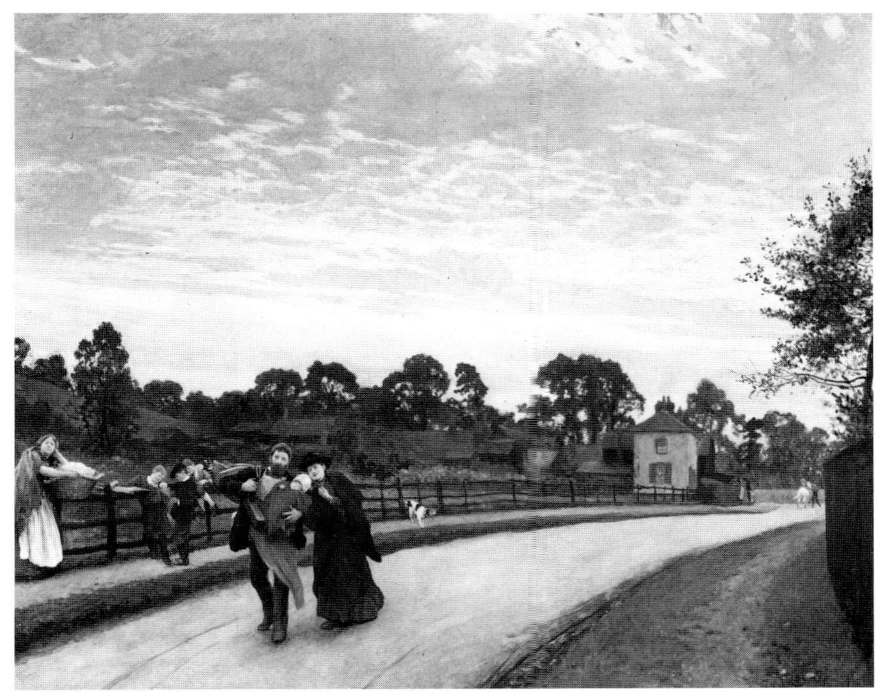

Plate 35

HUBERT VON HERKOMER (1849–1914)

*THE FIRST BORN*, 1887

Oil on canvas, 44 × 56″

From his native Bavaria, Hubert von Herkomer moved with his family to England while still a child and later studied art in both London and Munich. He contributed scores of paintings, many of them portraits, to the Royal Academy between 1869–1904, and he was well known both for his illustrations for *The Graphic* and for his often riveting images of contemporary poverty and old age.

When it was exhibited in 1887, *The First Born* was rightly compared with the style and sentiment of the artist's friend Frederick Walker. Basically a rather idyllic celebration of life, the painting includes a trio of young boys whose presence suggests a later stage of youthful development. The setting is probably the village of Bushey, where Herkomer often painted. The father strides along confidently, carrying a carpenter's plane under one arm, his baby in the other, and this plus the somewhat halo-like swaddling behind the infant's head may suggest that the group can be interpreted as a rustic equivalent of the Holy Family.

Plate 36

GEORGE HARVEY (1806–1876)

*THE PENNY BANK*, 1864

Oil on canvas, 42 × 60″

One of the original associates of the Royal Scottish Academy in 1826, George Harvey later exhibited at the Royal Academy and elsewhere but remained best known for the patriotic and religious subjects he sent to the Scottish institution.

*The Penny Bank*, exhibited at the Royal Scottish Academy in 1864, includes a lively cast of characters who await their turn with the "banker." Such penny banks existed for the benefit of the poor, as did mutual benefit societies of Christmas clubs. Here a man with a ledger sits at a makeshift table entering accounts, while a little dog stands guard near the safe and several young patrons crowd about with their pennies to deposit. The quarters are somewhat shabby and there is a 'to let" sign on the door down the hall, but this squalor has not deterred the queue of clients, among them a fishergirl counting her coins and, in the corridor, a few barefoot urchins gazing at a well-shod comrade who holds out some money for inspection.

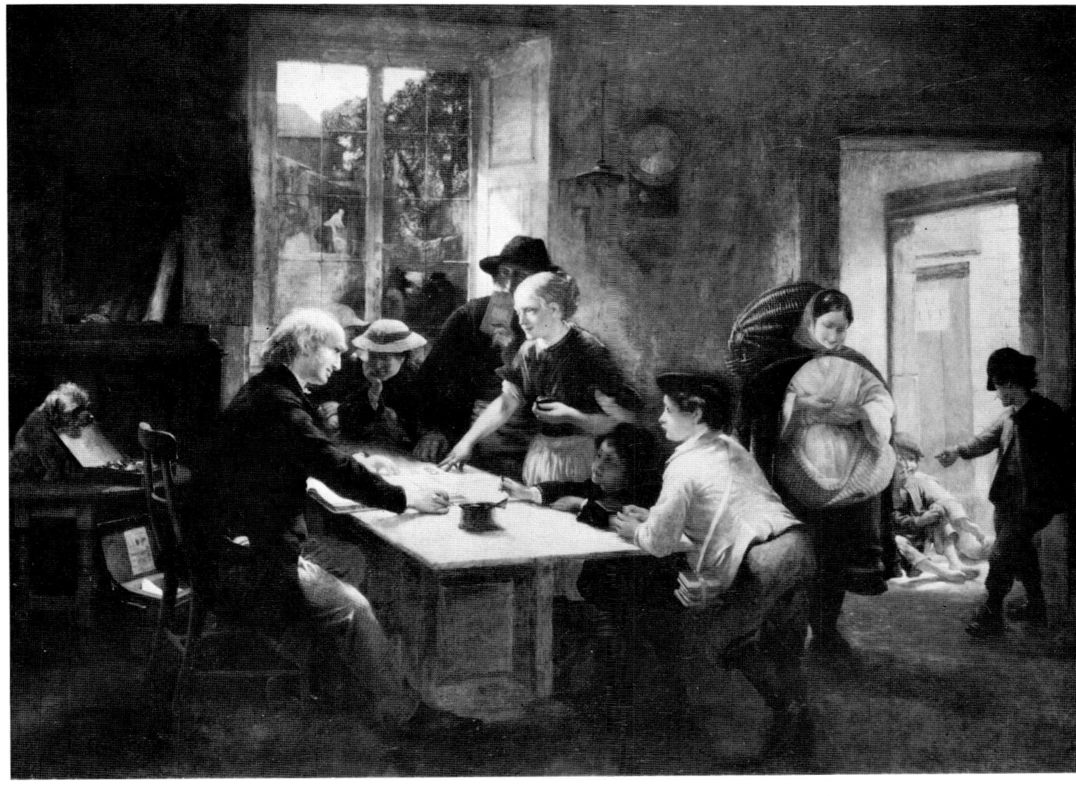

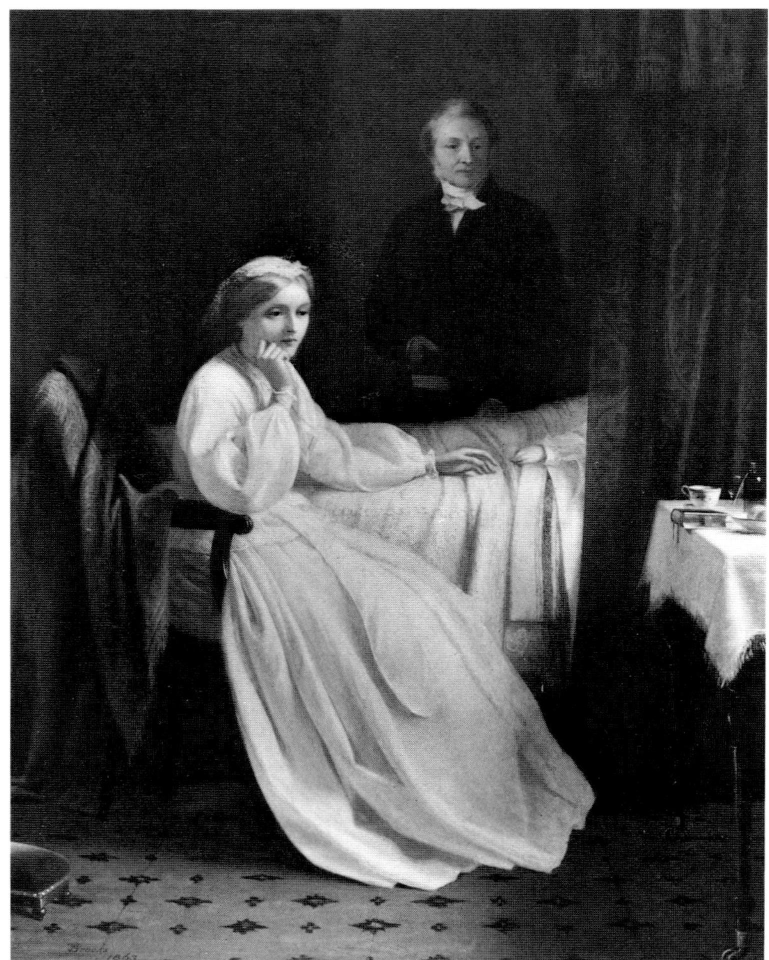

Plate 37

THOMAS BROOKS (1818–1891)

*RESIGNATION*, 1863

Oil on canvas, 36 ×27″

Educated initially in London at Sass's Art School, Thomas Brooks first earned a living as a portrait painter before turning to historical and genre subjects. By 1872 nearly forty of his works had been made into engravings, and the merits of his pictures, as an *Art-Journal* critic pointed out that year, were "not overlooked by the public . . . in the substantial way of patronage."

Some of Brooks's early subjects included Scottish scenes of cottage life or literature, but he also produced numerous canvases that dealt with the trials of motherhood and womankind in general, such as *The Mother's Dream*, 1852, and *The Awakened Conscience*, 1853. Moreover, he painted several deathbed scenes, and two sorrowful vignettes of 1859–60, *Consolation* and *Faith*, that depict sick or dying young women.

*Resignation* was accompanied by some lines from a poem by Henry Wadsworth Longfellow which underscore how the deceased child (whose hand only is visible) had ". . . gone unto that school/Where she no longer needs our poor protection,/And Christ himself doth rule." This is one of many Victorian melancholic canvases, and here a minister stands near a sad mother, who stares at a tabletop still life of a Bible, medicine, and untouched food.

Plate 38

THOMAS COOPER GOTCH (1854–1931)

*ALLELUYA*, ca. 1896

Oil on canvas, 20 ×26¼″

Thomas Gotch is often mentioned as an English symbolist, but he was also affiliated with the Newlyn School and married a fellow art student, Caroline Yates. Influenced, perhaps, by Italian fifteenth-century representations of female saints, Gotch held rather personal, liberal views about women and around the turn of the century produced numerous canvases of female "deities," dewy-eyed, decorative women or girls often literally enshrined amid sumptuous fabrics and settings.

*Alleluya* may be a study for (or a reduced detail of) a large canvas at the Tate of the same title that was accompanied by lines from Psalms xlvii. 6 and 7. The two angelic girls in this small version appear among the choristers in the Tate picture; they seem to wear costumes of different eras and nationalities, thus perhaps reinforcing *The Athenaeum's* belief that this variety of attire—from medieval to Oriental to modern—was intended as a comment on the universality of praises sung in worship of God.

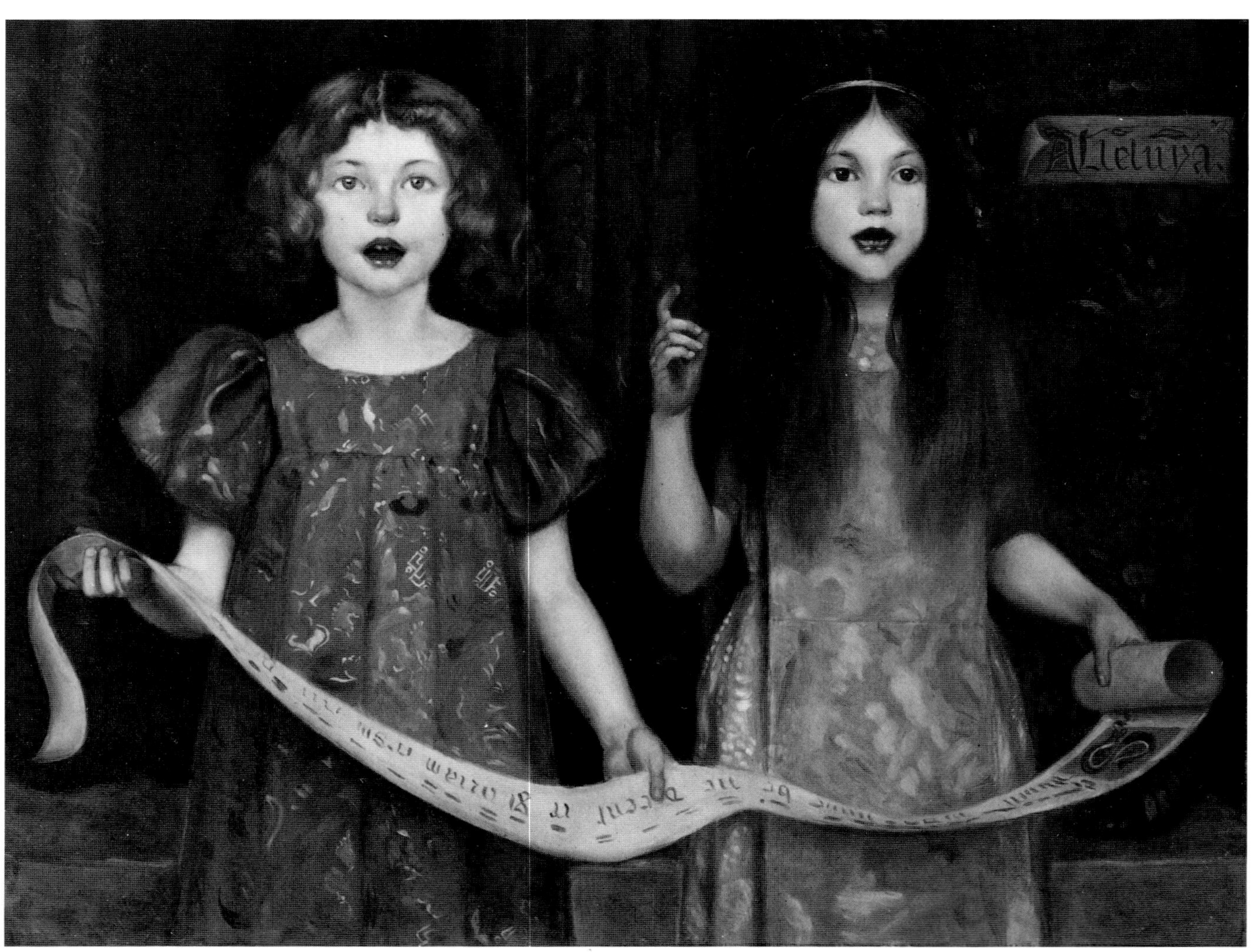

Plate 39

GEORGE ELGAR HICKS (1824–1914)

## *A CLOUD WITH A SILVER LINING,* 1890

Oil on canvas, 49½ × 40″

Entering the Royal Academy schools in 1844, George Hicks went on to produce scores of pictures for the annual exhibitions there during the years 1848–1903. Many of his early paintings focused on the theme of the child, including *Infant Baptism,* 1850, and *Mother and Child,* 1873.

*A Cloud with a Silver Lining* is not a typical late work of the artist and may in fact reflect autobiographical details from the artist's life many years earlier. Hicks wrote that the painting was conceived when he contracted smallpox in 1850, followed a few years later by the deaths of two sons. In this canvas of 1890, the setting is a humble interior where two parents bend over the lifeless form of their little one. The father has removed his crude workboots so as not to disturb the sick child, and the plant on the windowsill is typically an index in Victorian narrative pictures of the health of the inhabitant. Much of the composition is dominated by the arrival of a winged angel, who escorts the vigorous and healthy spirit of the dead child into another sphere to join its heavenly father. The composition is reminiscent of the religious iconography of both the pietà and the adoration of the newborn Christ, and Hicks himself was apparently quite devout.

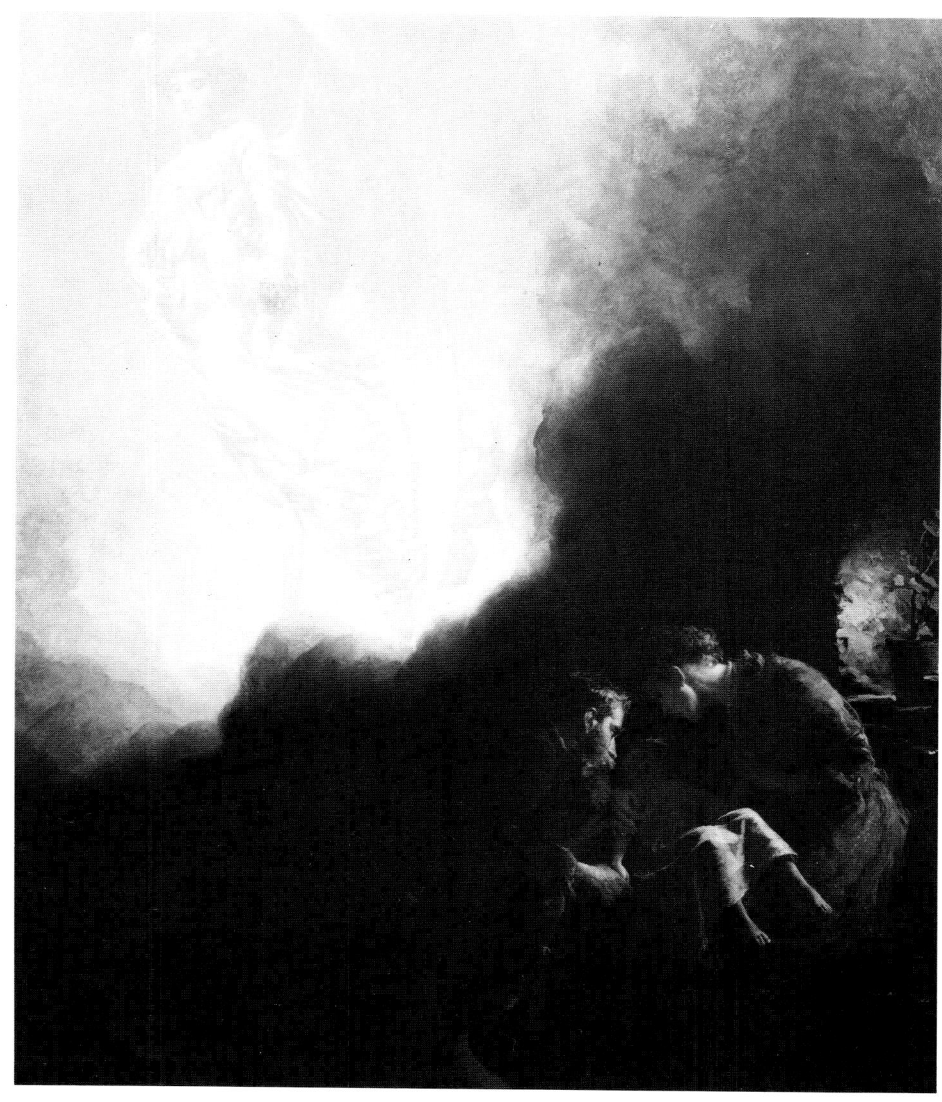

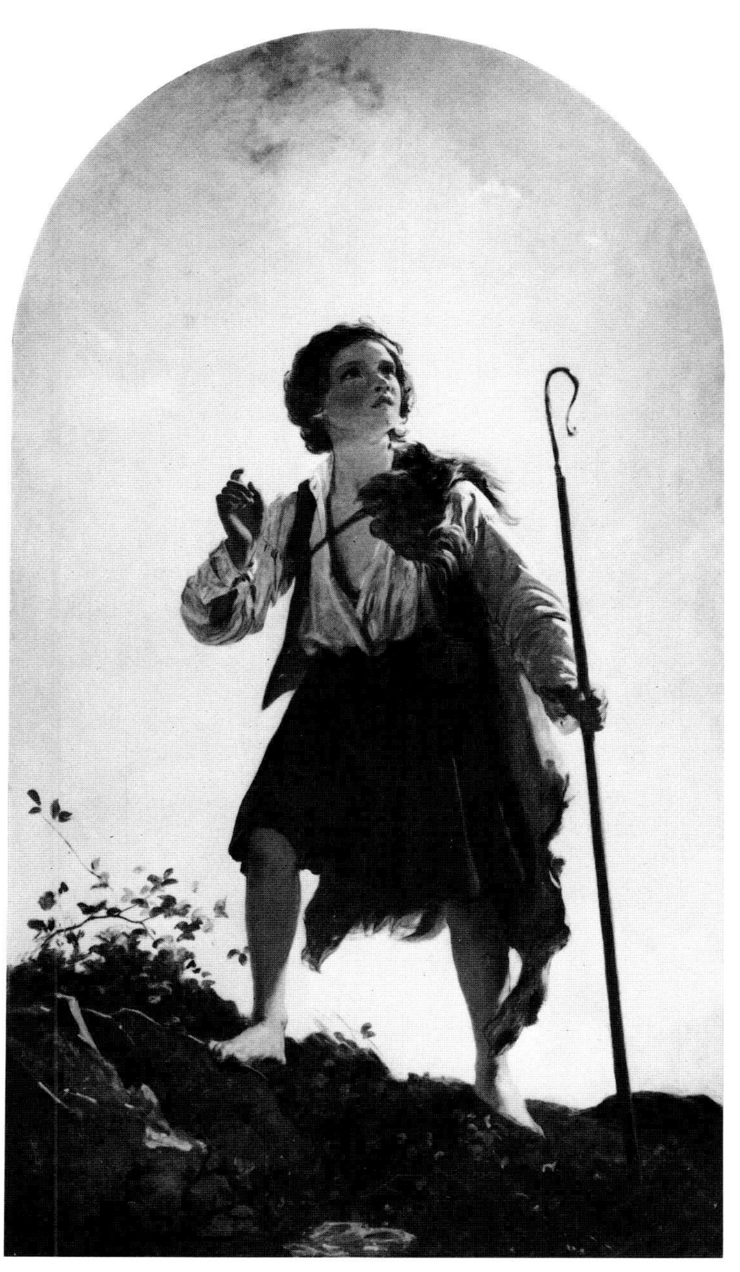

Plate 40

JAMES SANT (1820–1916)

## *IT IS THE LARK! THE HERALD OF THE MORN,* 1880s?

Oil on canvas (arched top), 84 × 47″

James Sant almost immediately established himself as a portraitist, becoming a favorite among the aristocracy and painting such sitters as the Prince Consort, the Duchess of Marlborough, and other members of the royal family. He exhibited numerous genre pictures (many with children as the main subject) in addition to scores of portraits at the Royal Academy in particular.

*It is the Lark!* combines certain qualities of a portrait with a literary or domestic subject. In other large-scale portraits of boys Sant often showed the figures in costume and with somewhat soulful expressions, and this is probably another romanticized likeness of a young aristocrat masquerading as a shepherd. Queen Victoria admired Scottish garb and dressed her own sons in tartan kilts, and perhaps this youth wears his clan's tartan.

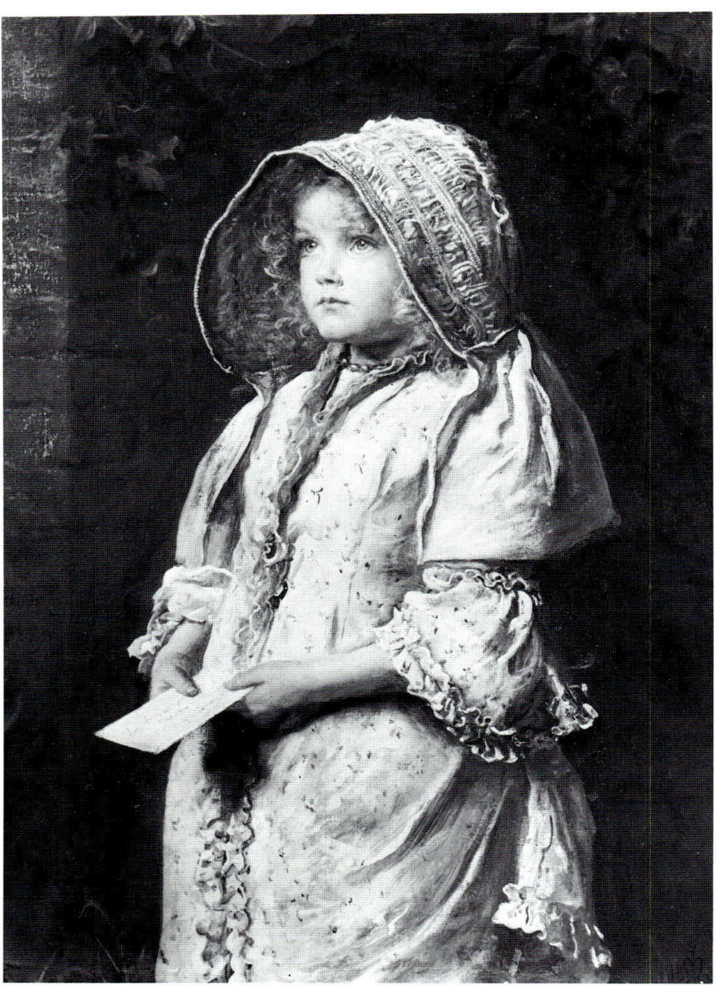

*(Front Cover)*

## JOHN EVERETT MILLAIS (1829–1896)

## *FOR THE SQUIRE*, 1882

Oil on canvas, 33½ ×25″

John Everett Millais was a true artistic prodigy, entering the Royal Academy schools in 1840 and winning a gold medal there when he was only about eighteen. At the Academy he became friendly with Holman Hunt, and the pair formed, with Dante Gabriel Rossetti and others, the famous and radical group of youthful artists known as the Pre-Raphaelite Brotherhood.

*For the Squire* was exhibited at the Grosvenor Gallery in 1883 and follows in a tradition of images of winsome and picturesque girls produced by Millais in the late 1870s and 1880s, including *Cherry Ripe*, 1879, *Une Grande Dame*, 1883, and *The Nest*, 1887. Sometimes Millais used his own daughter, sometimes friends or professional models as sitters, but the identity of the girl here is not known. A rosy-cheeked, dewy-eyed country lass, she is shown almost trembling as she proffers a letter to the unseen male squire, the principal landowner in a village or country district who was perceived as a symbol of authority by tenant farmers (and presumably by viewers of the painting). Rather loosely but fluently painted in a style quite different from early Pre-Raphaelitism, *For the Squire* owes a pictorial debt to Millais's 1852 *A Huguenot*; in that early and influential painting the presence of a stone wall with foliage creates a patterned backdrop of bricks and ivy that serves rather beautifully to seal off the protagonists from the outside world As one of the most important and successful English artists of his time, Millais had many engravings of his works, including *For the Squire*, circulated throughout the world.

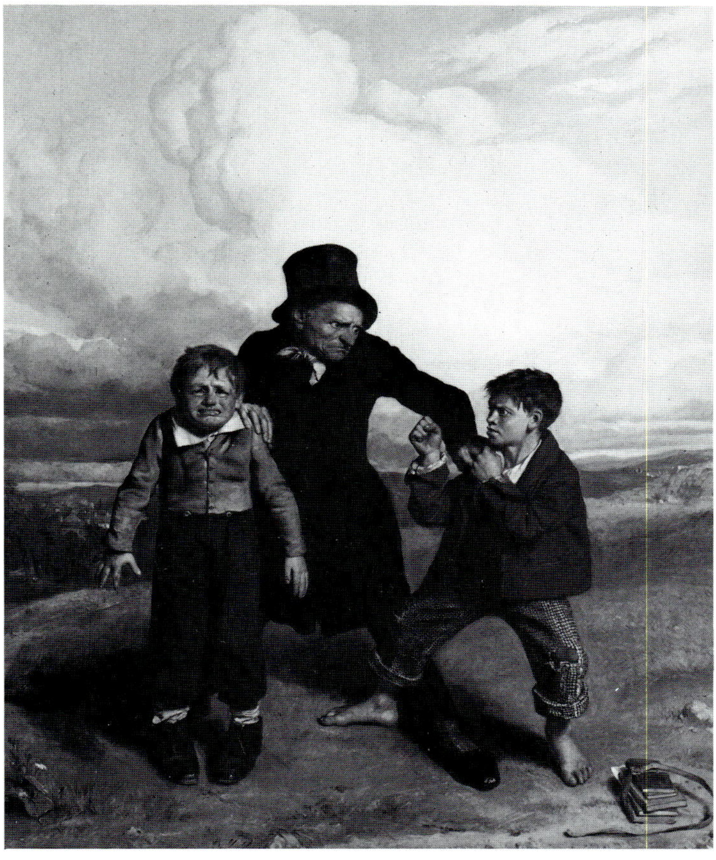

*(Back cover)*

## JOHN FAED (1820–1902)

## *BOYHOOD*, 1849

Oil on canvas, 41¾ ×33½″

The eldest of three artistic brothers, John Faed exhibited over two hundred paintings at the Royal Scottish Academy and also submitted works to the Royal Academy in London from 1855 to 1893.

*Boyhood* was one of Faed's first departures from portraiture and was exhibited with *Fun* and *Curiosity* in the 1850 Royal Scottish Academy. All three works explored the theme of childhood, and *Boyhood* was immediately bought by an art association, probably for the purpose of being engraved. Here two combatants are separated by an older man who acts as an unofficial referee and glowers at the more aggressive of the fighters. The lads seem to be country schoolboys, one cocky and pugnacious and the other red-faced, with a bloodied nose, and on the verge of tears. While the facial expressions in particular may seem exaggerated to modern viewers, the humor of the situation is still readily apparent. Faed was himself apparently just as unruly a boy as the belligerent youth in *Boyhood*, but his talent surfaced early and by the age of nine he had begun to receive commissions for his miniatures.